doodle corner

ADULT COLORING BOOK

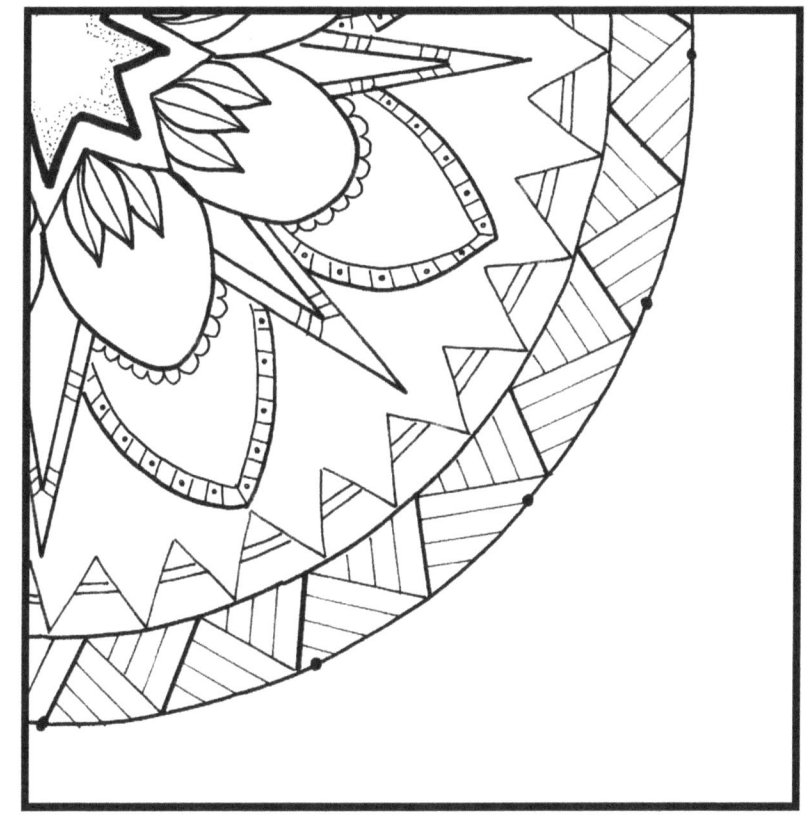

ILLUSTRATIONS BY
LOIDA B. TIU

Doodle Corner Adult Coloring Book Volume 1

Copyright

Copyright © 2015 by Loida B. Tiu

International Standard Book Number

ISBN-13: 978-1-519-18853-3
ISBN-10: 1-519-18853-6

For Information, please contact +63 9174753706

Or write to us doodlecorner2015@gmail.com

Printed in the United States of America

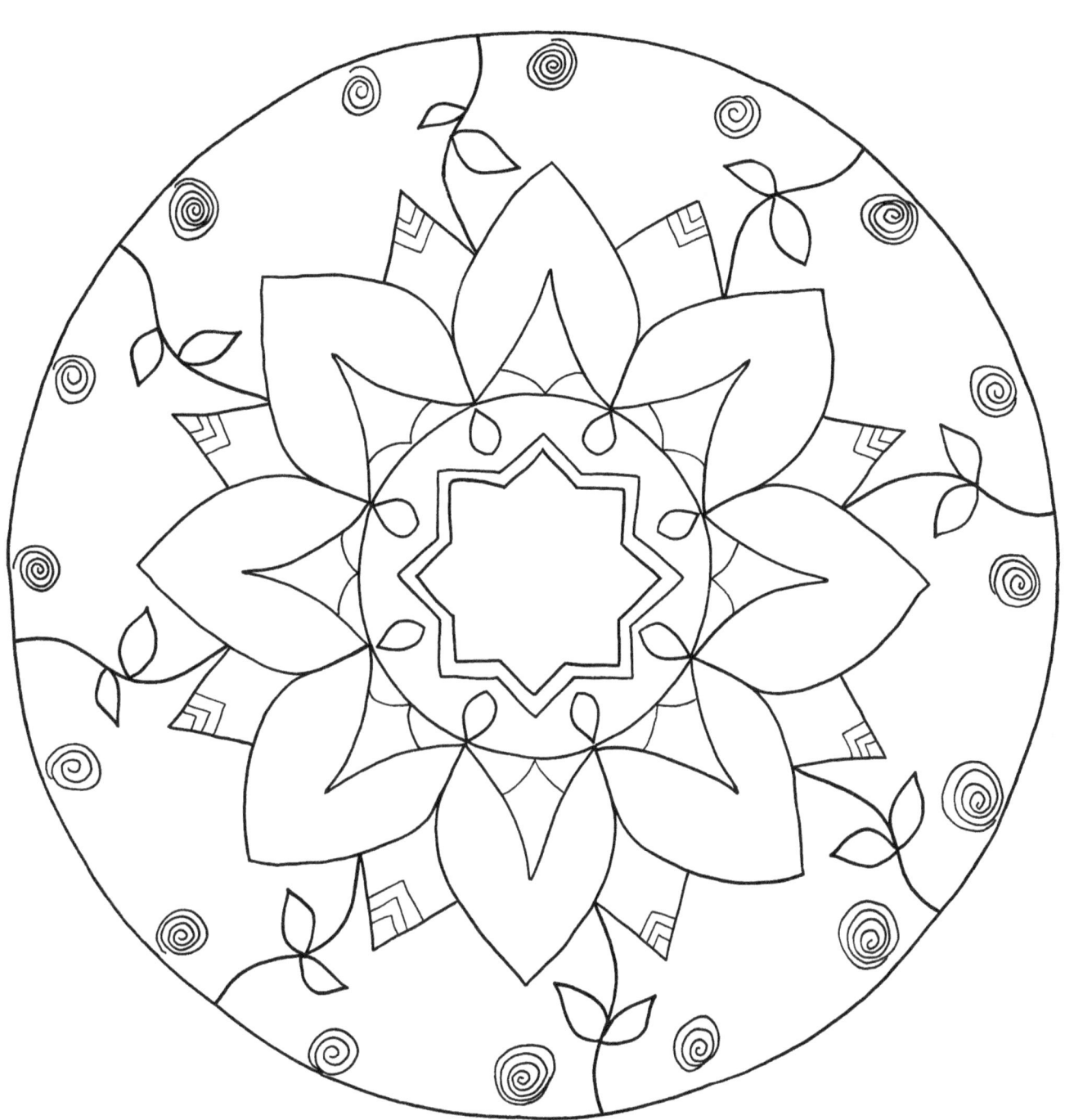

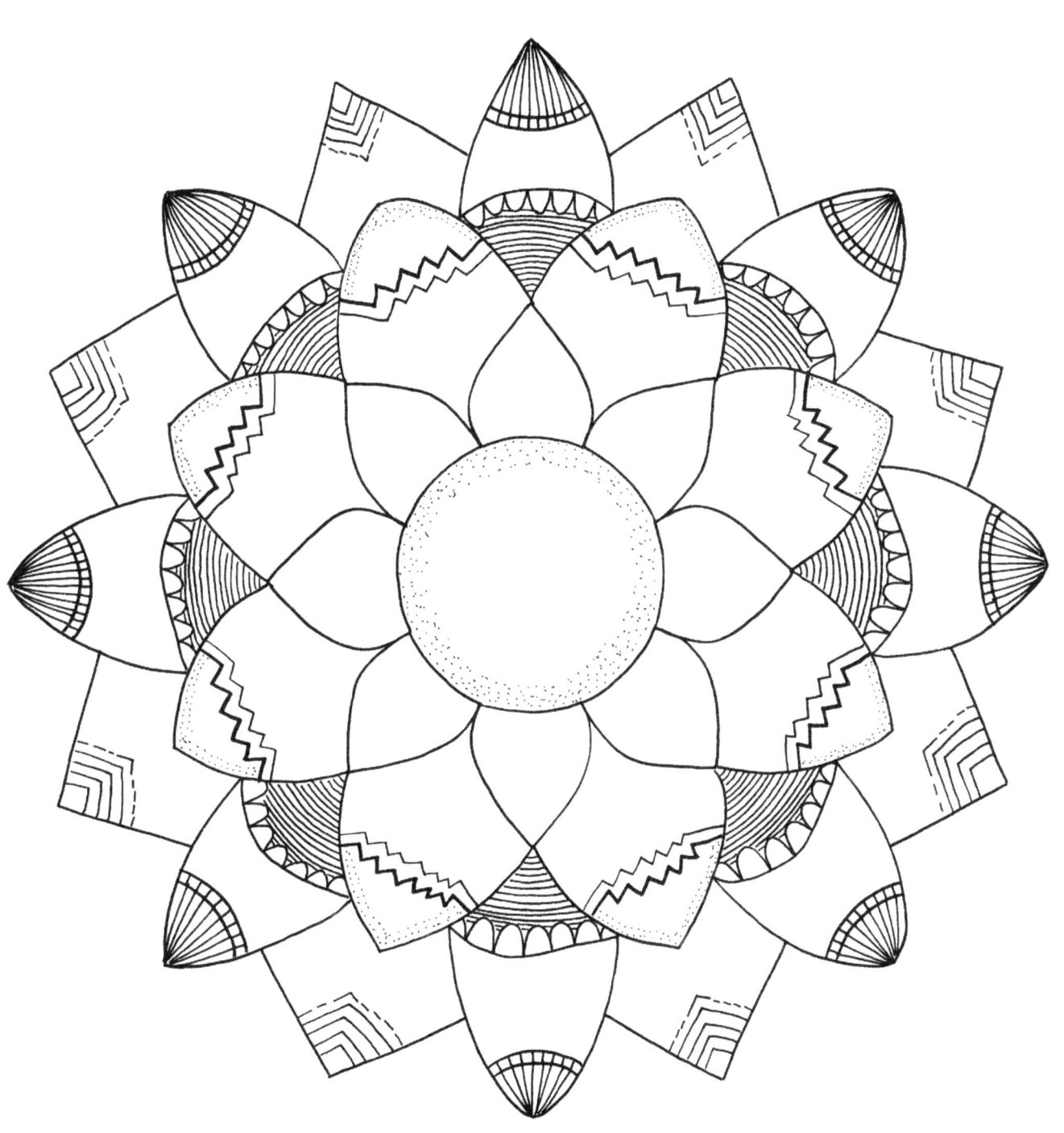

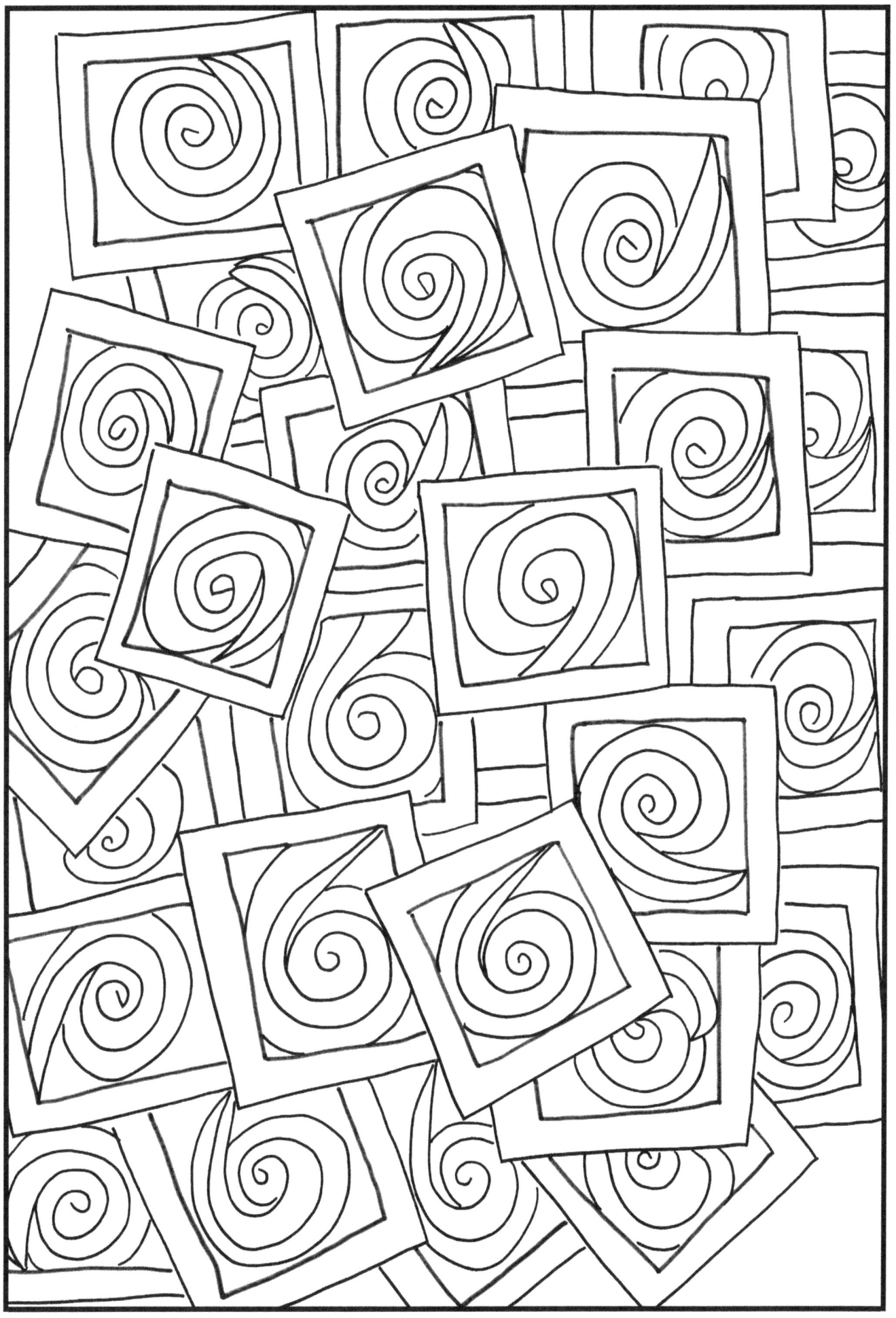

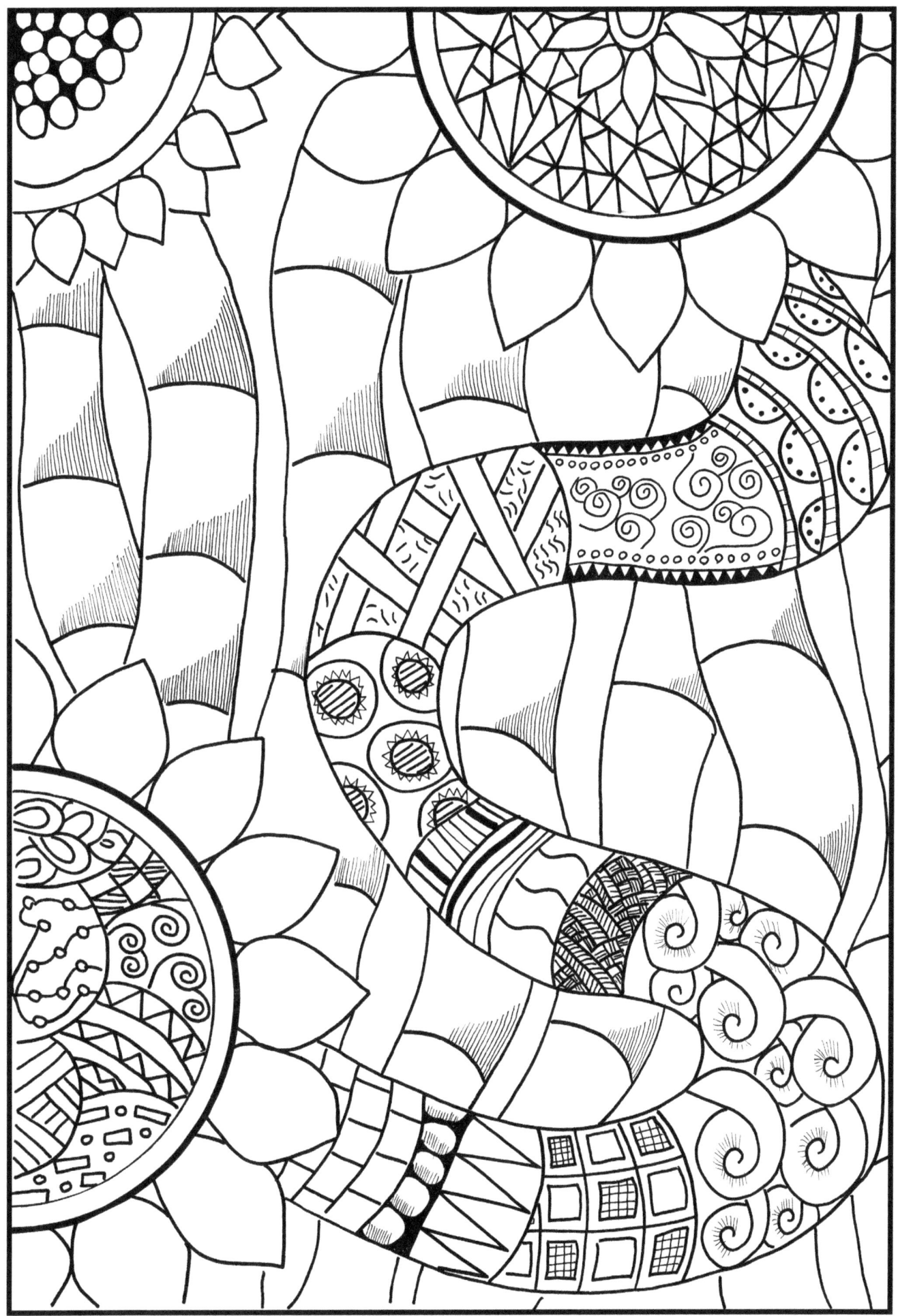

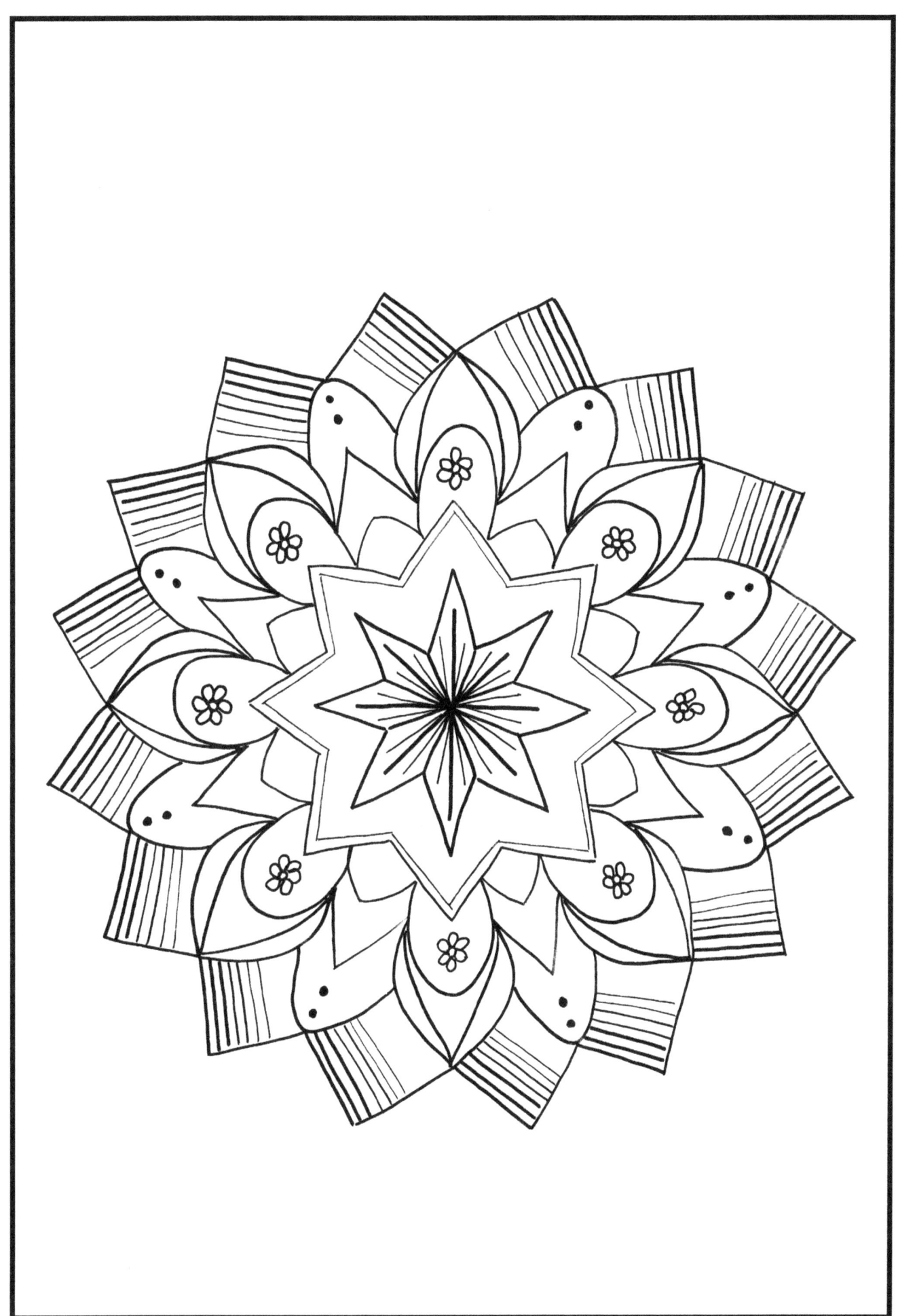

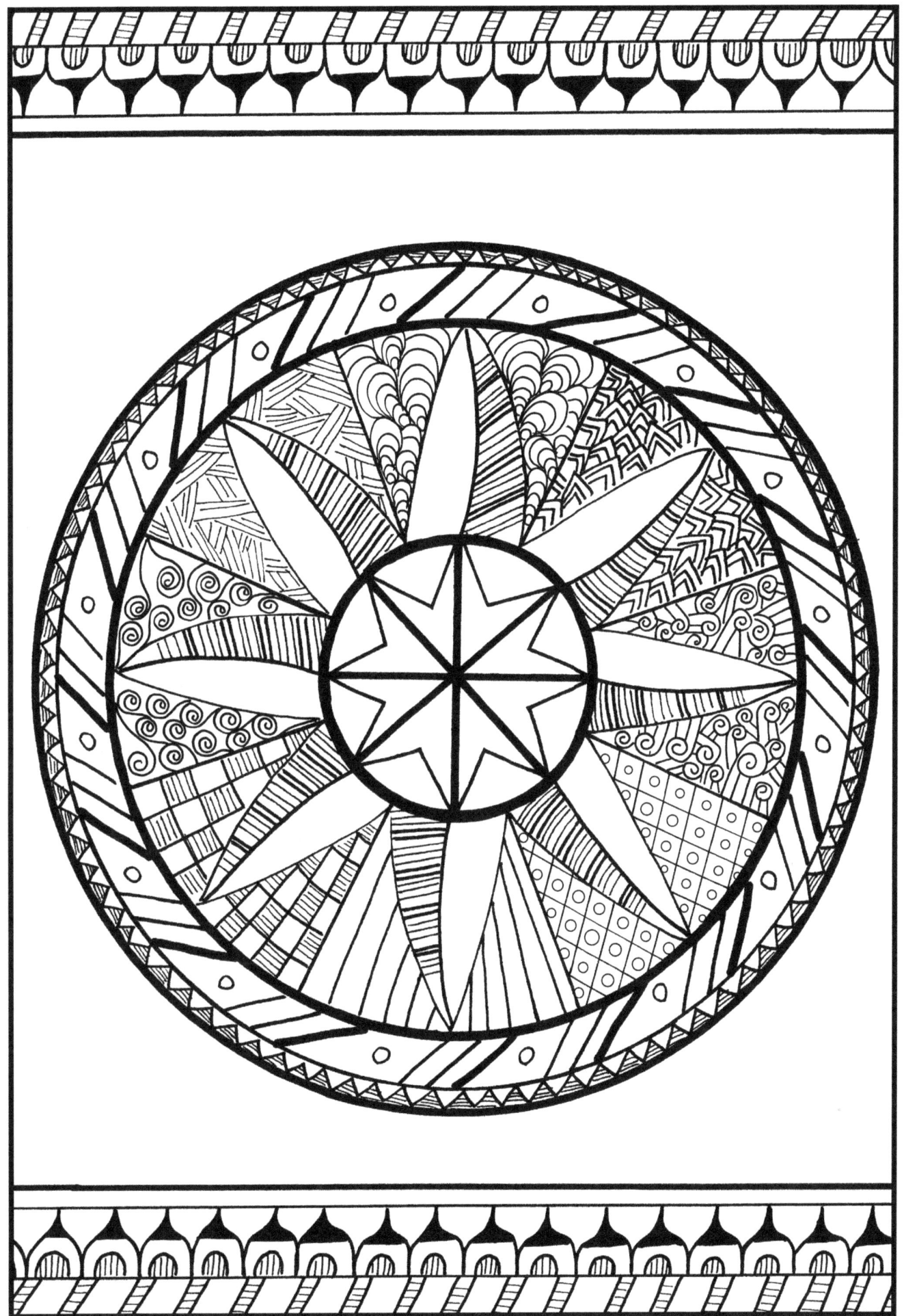

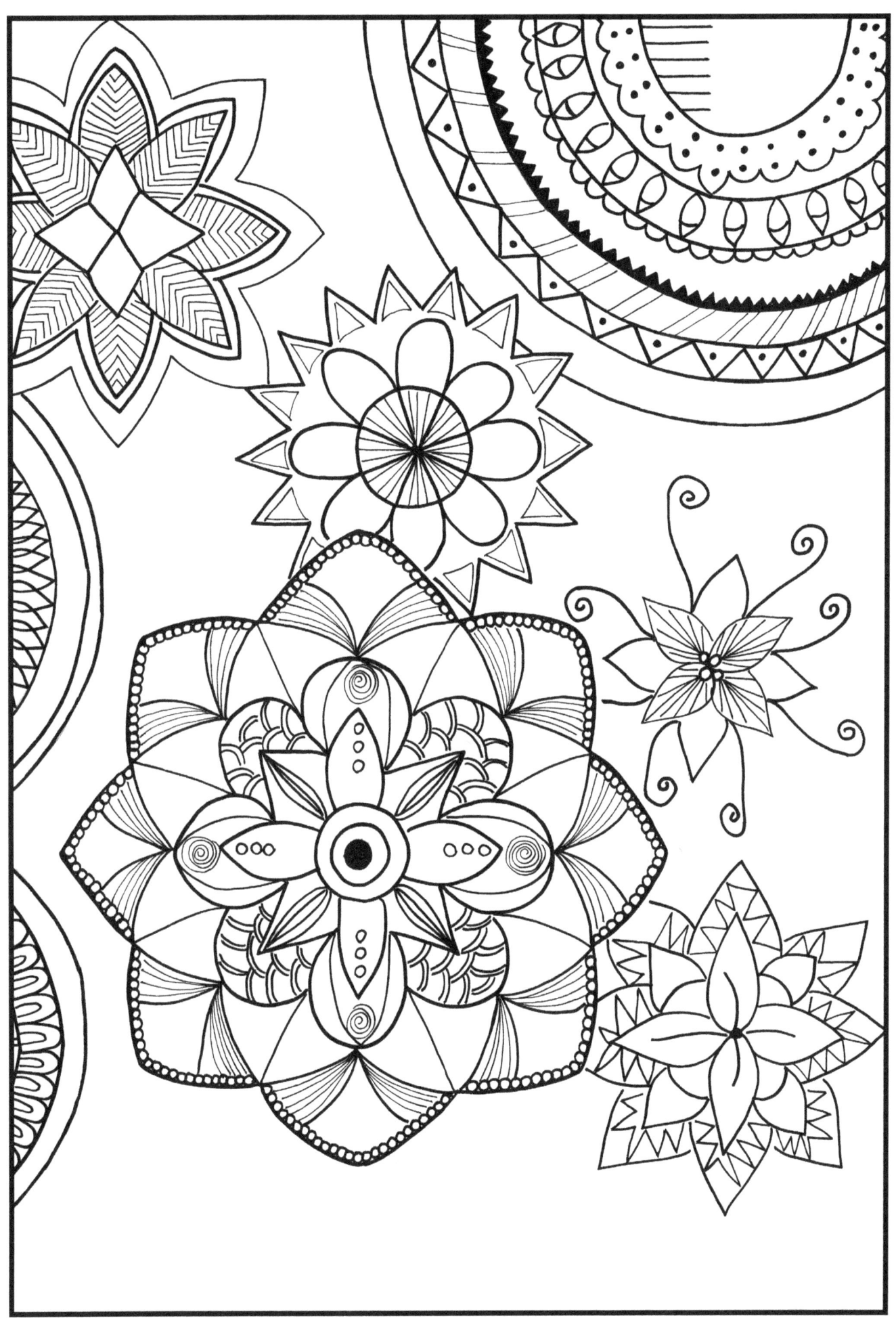

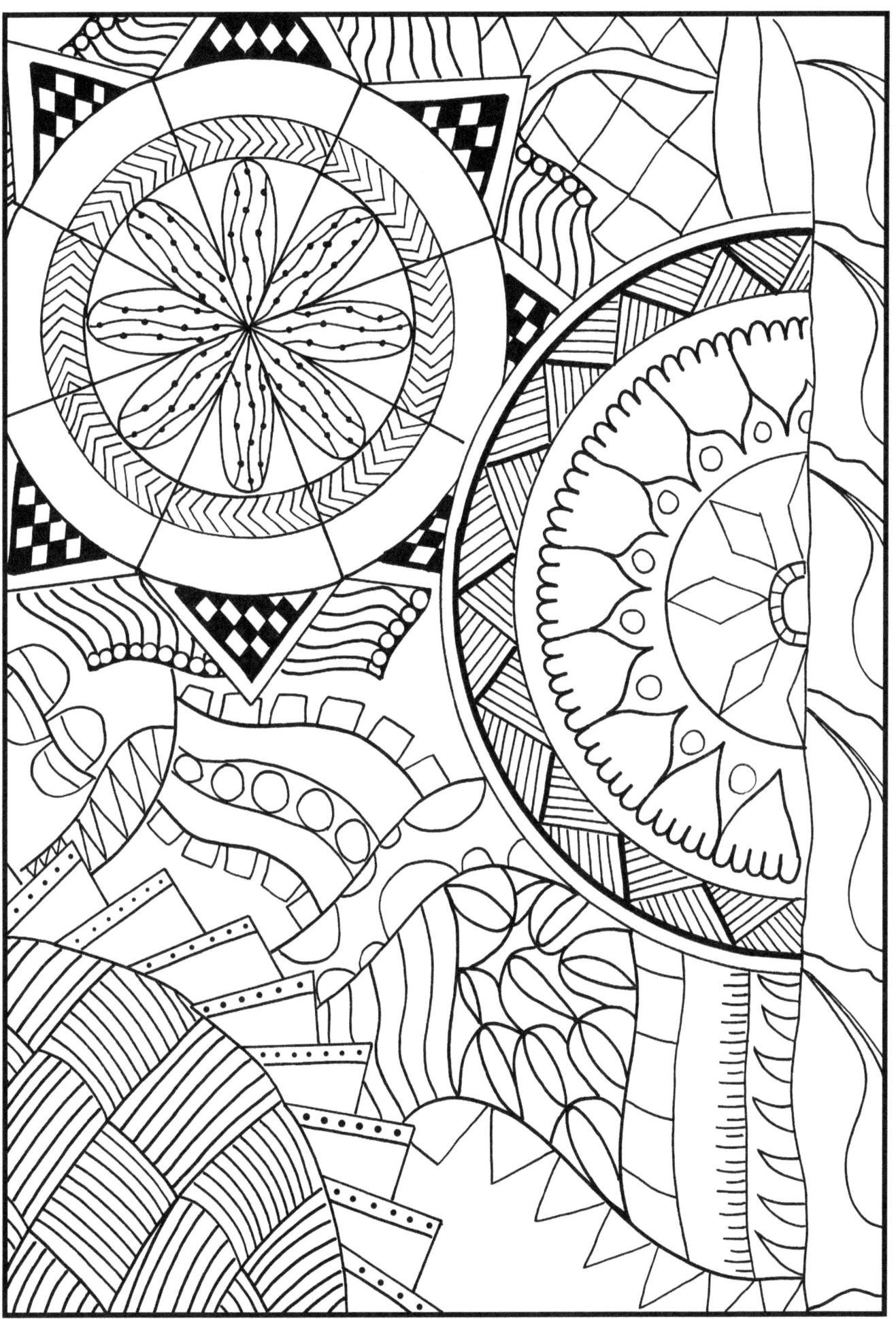

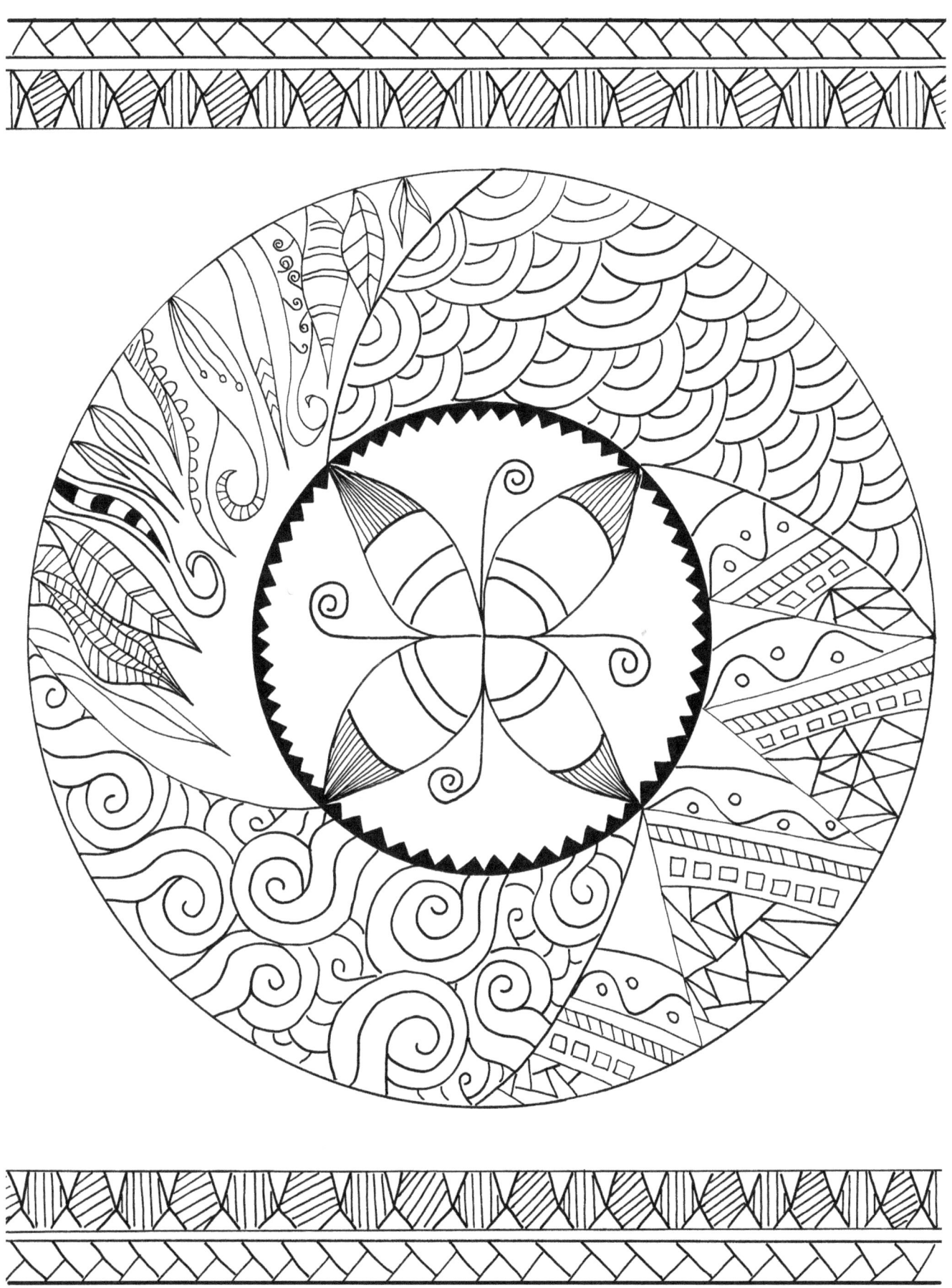

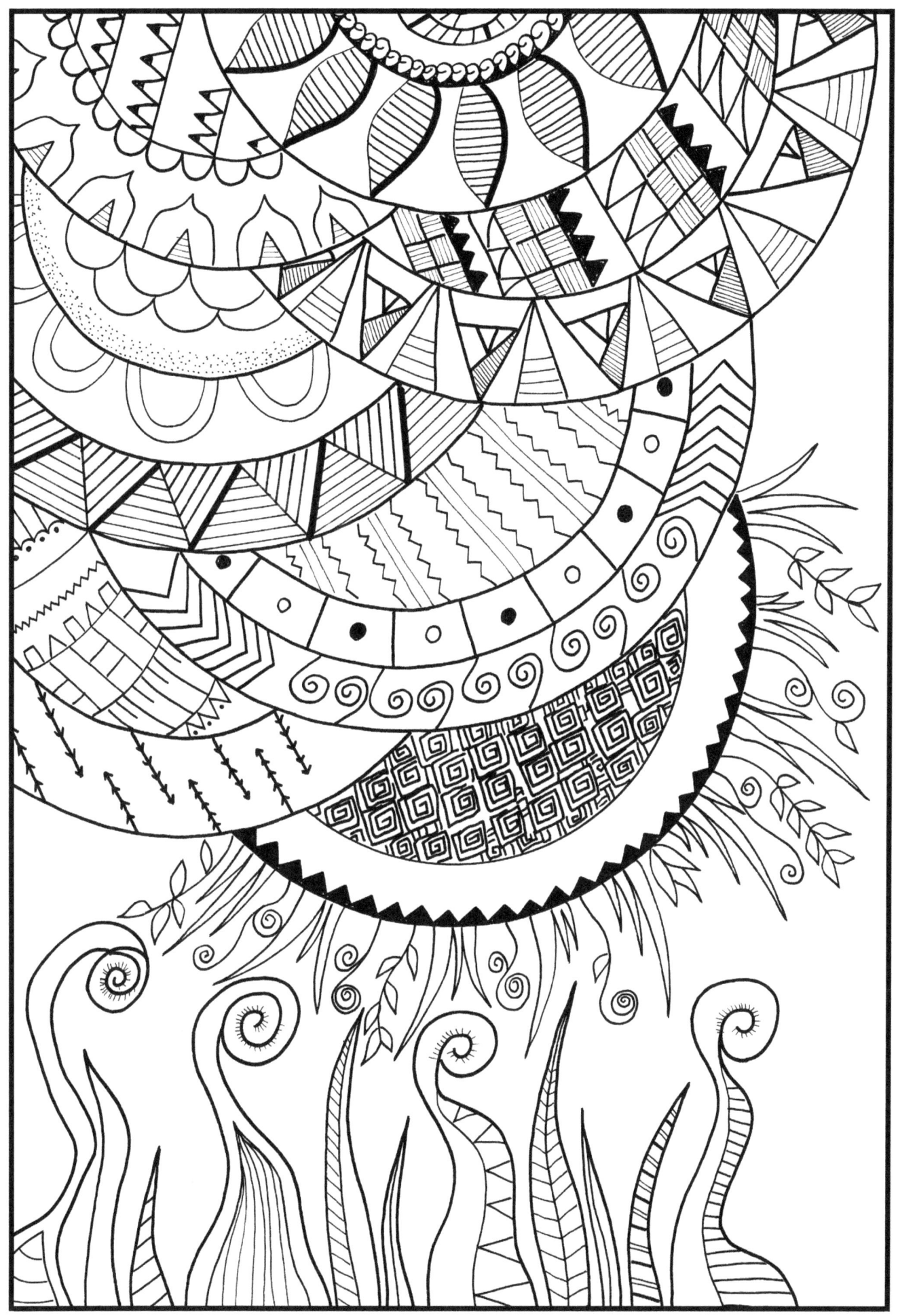

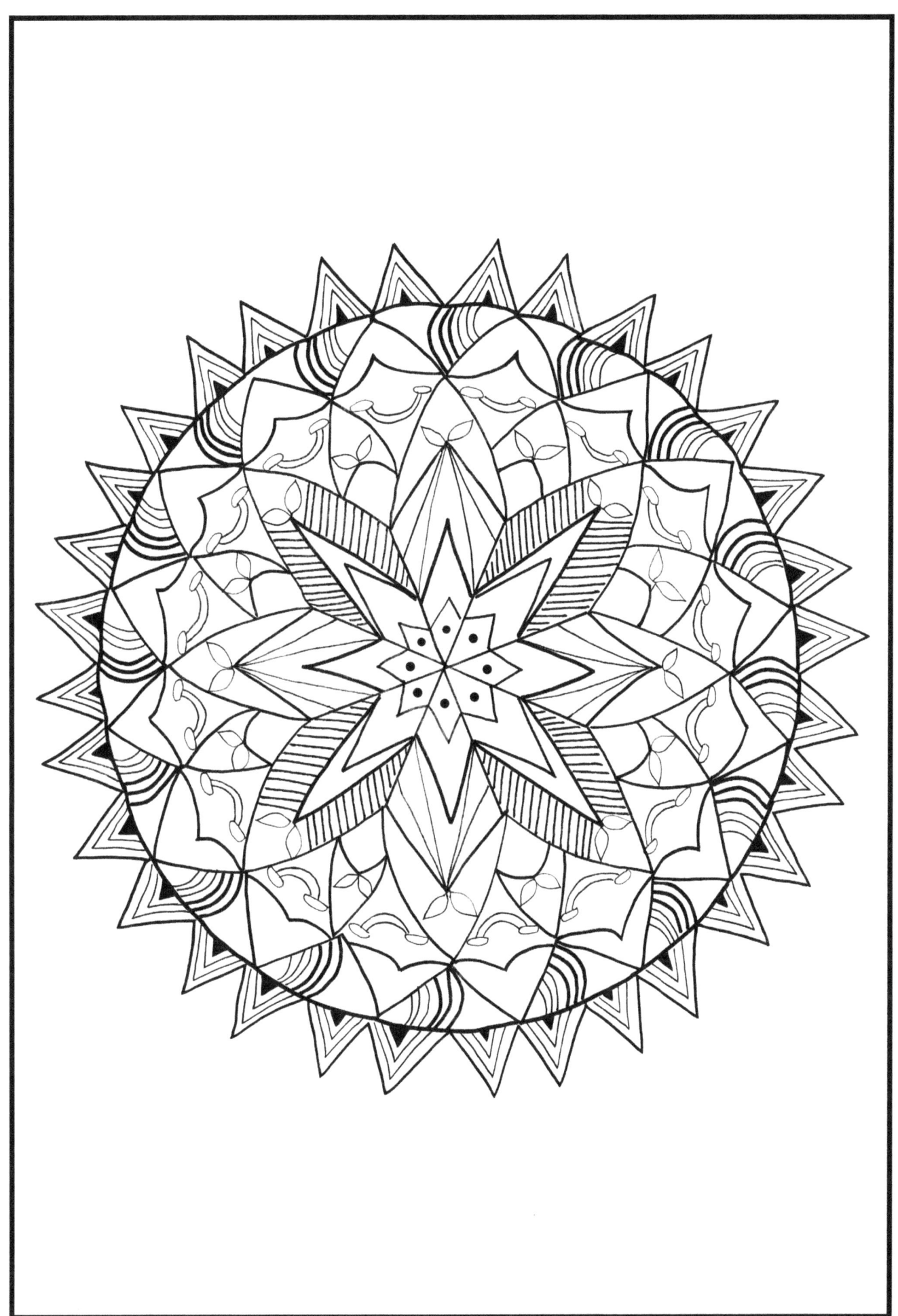

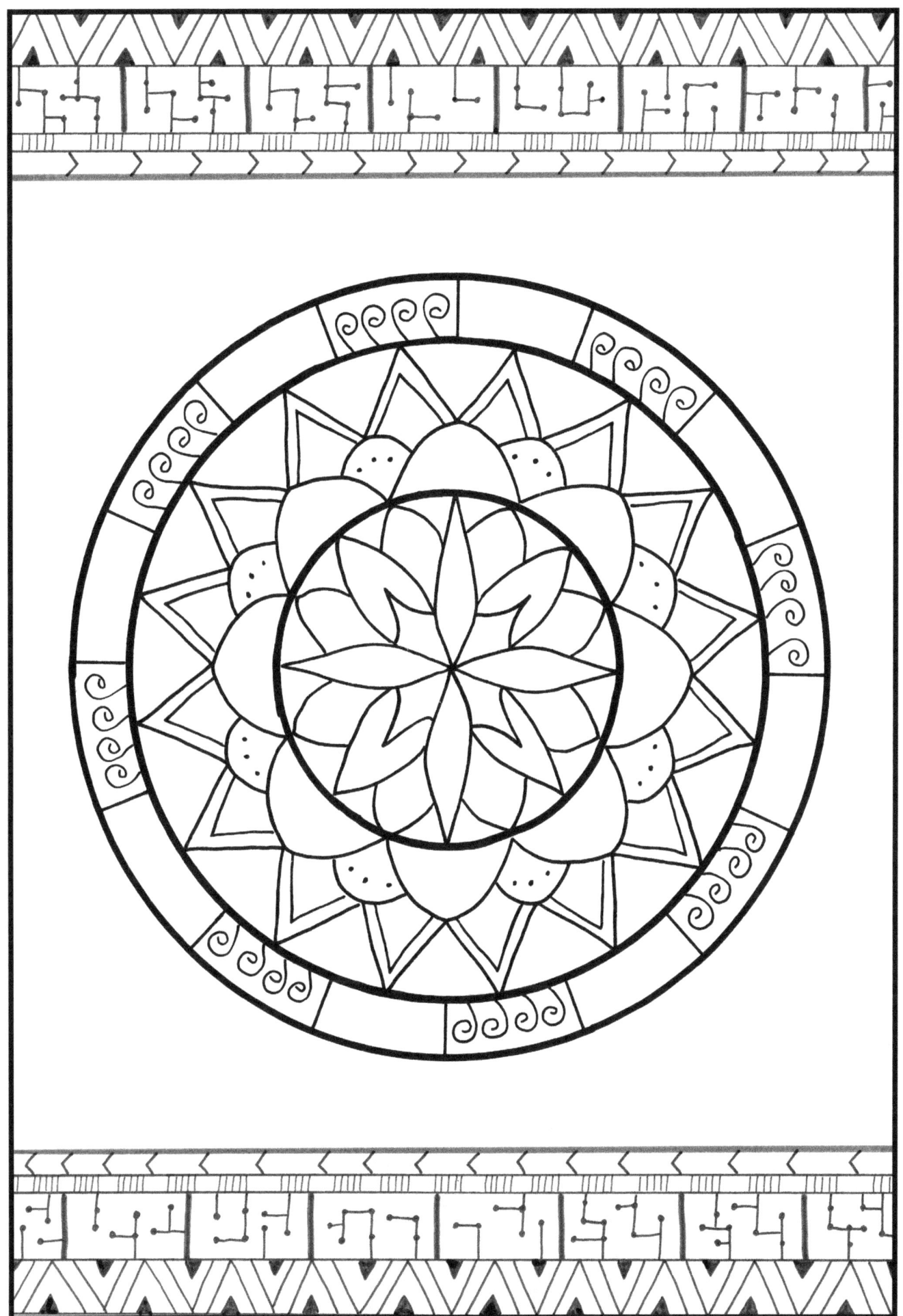

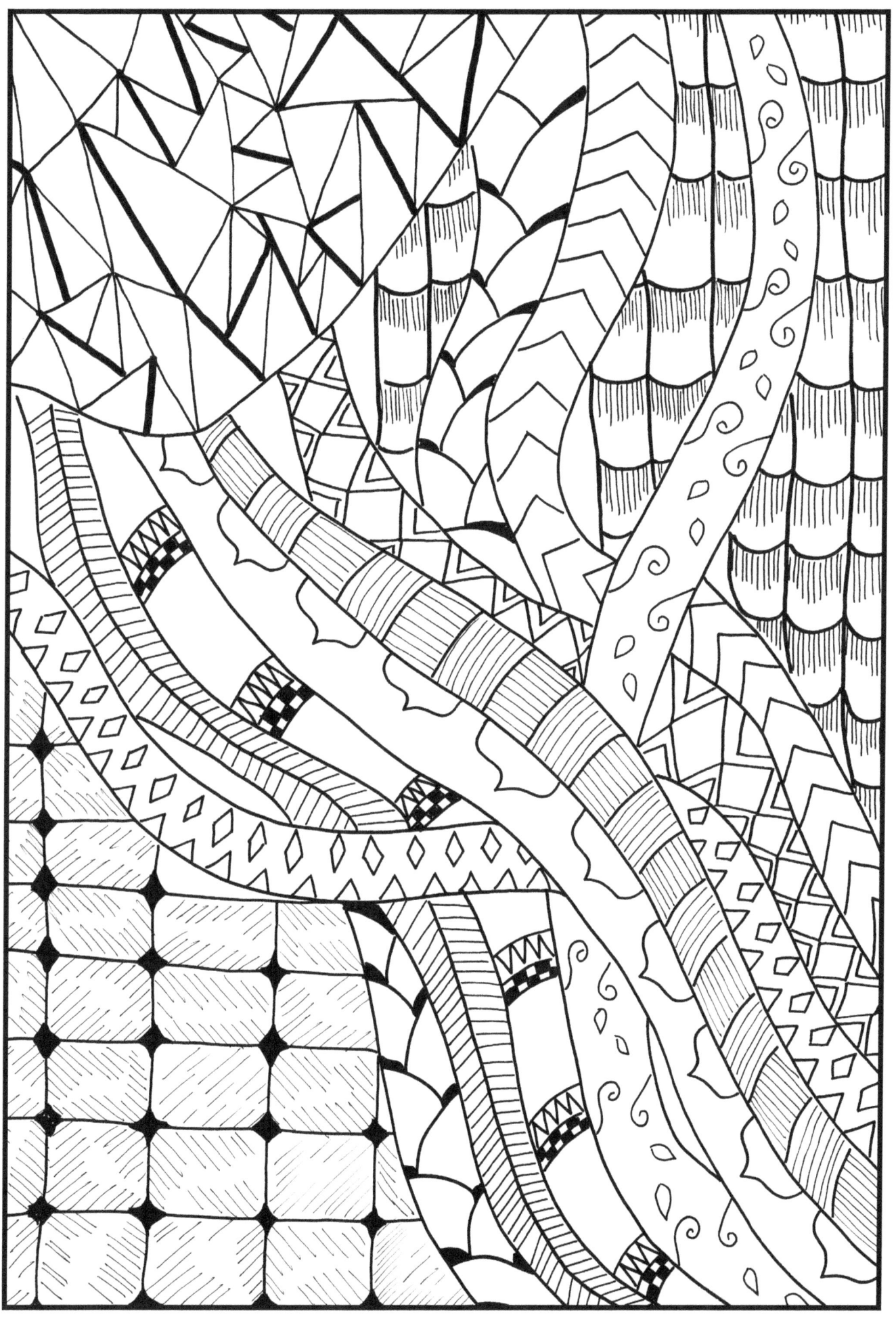

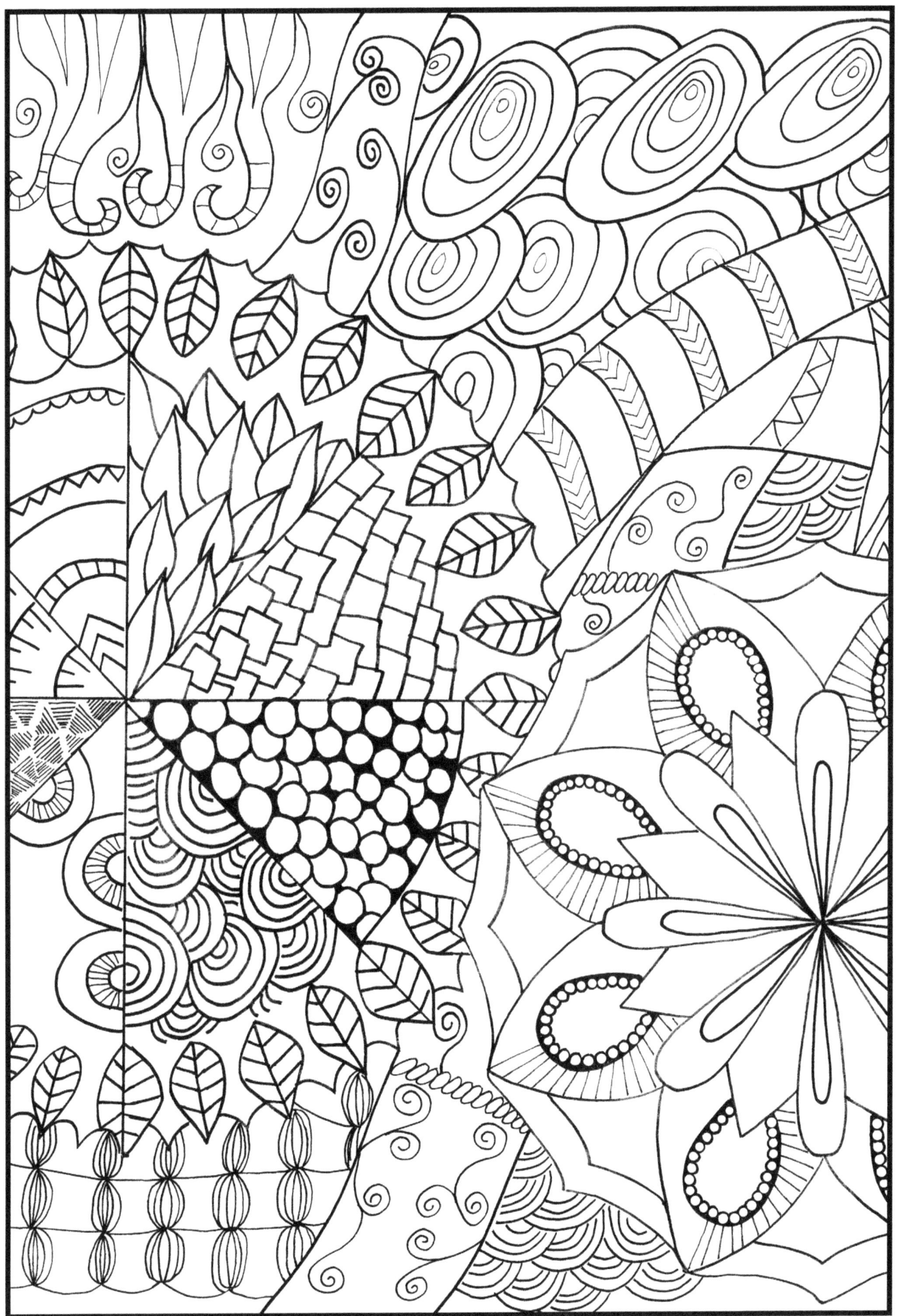

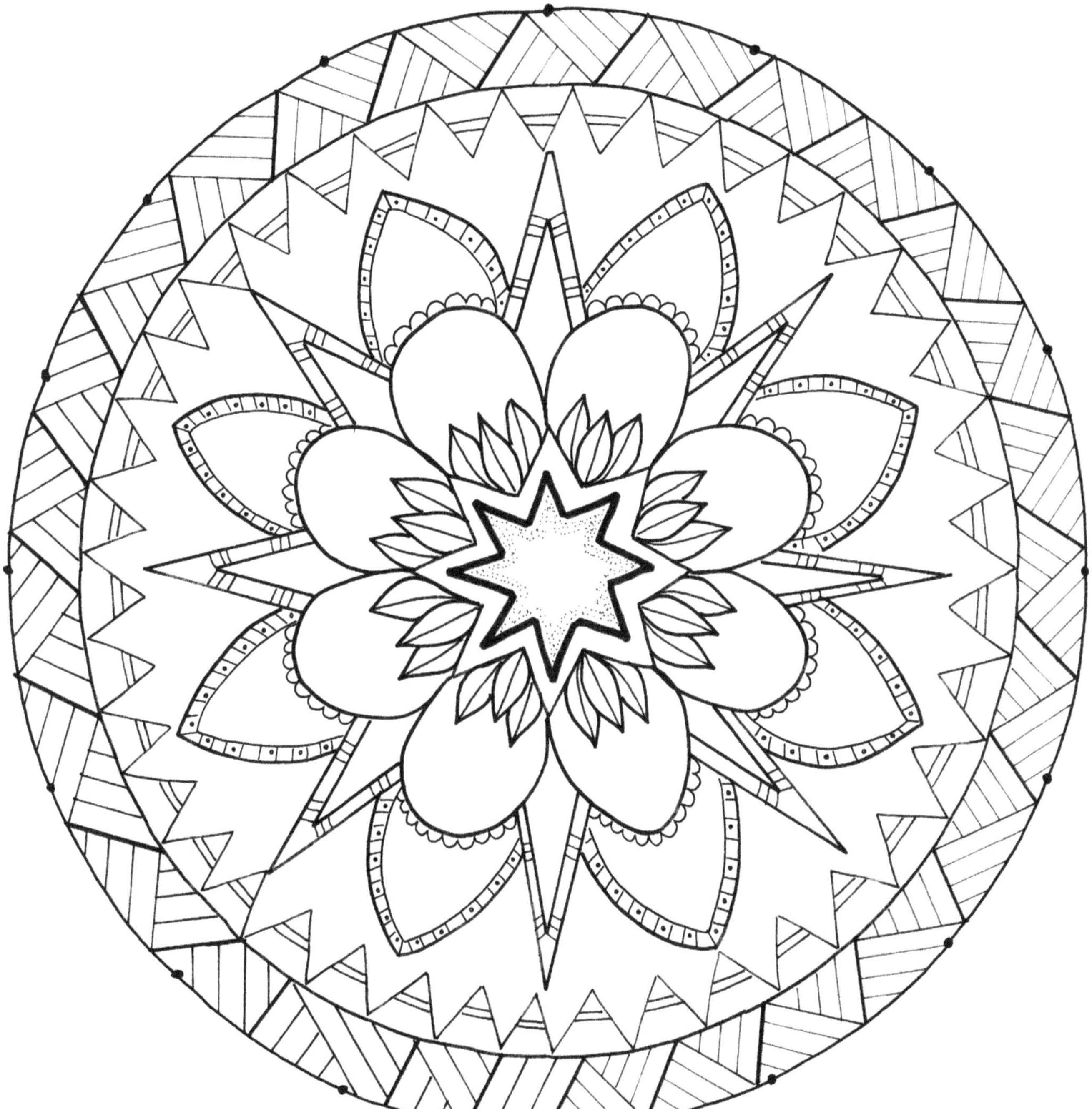

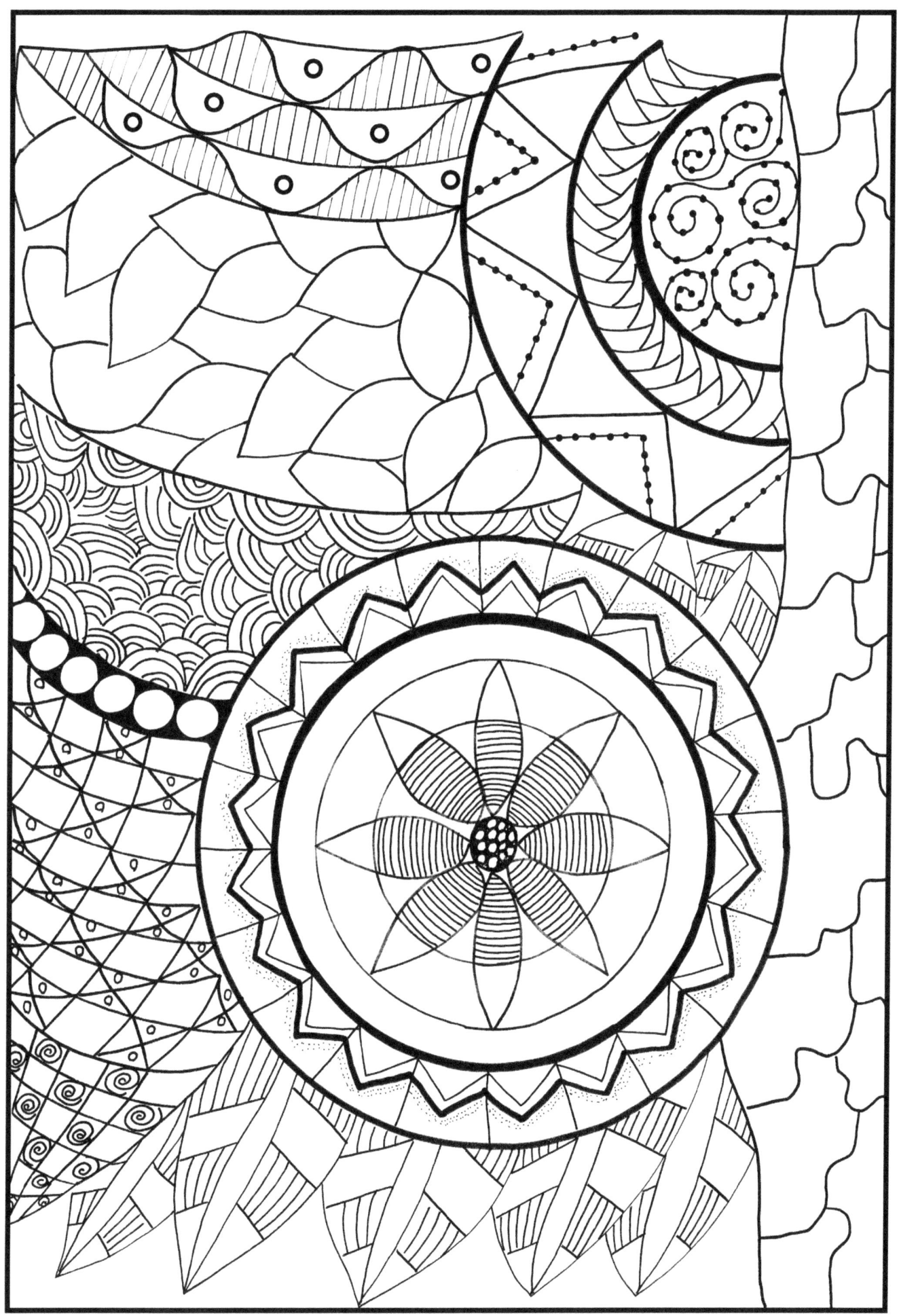

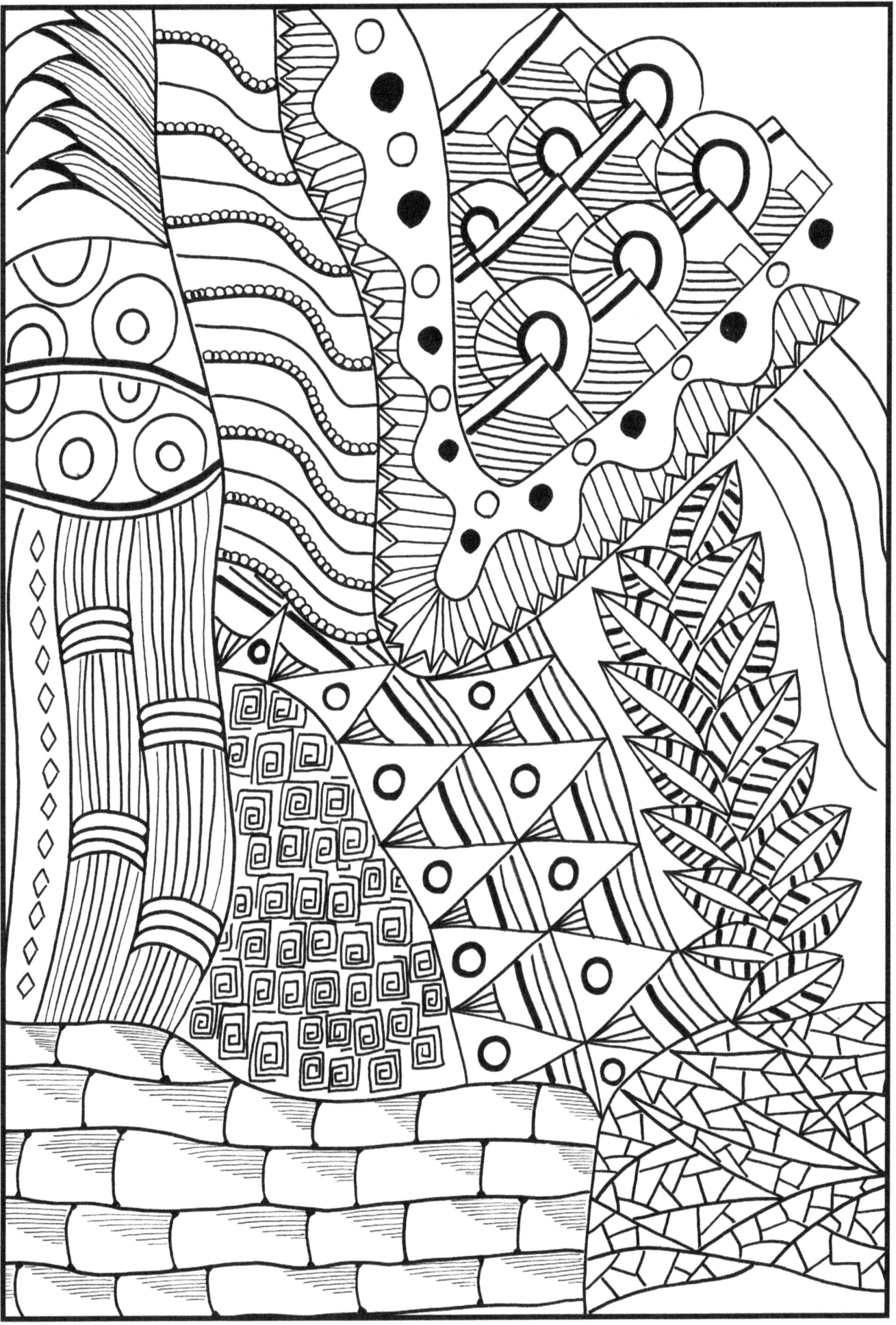

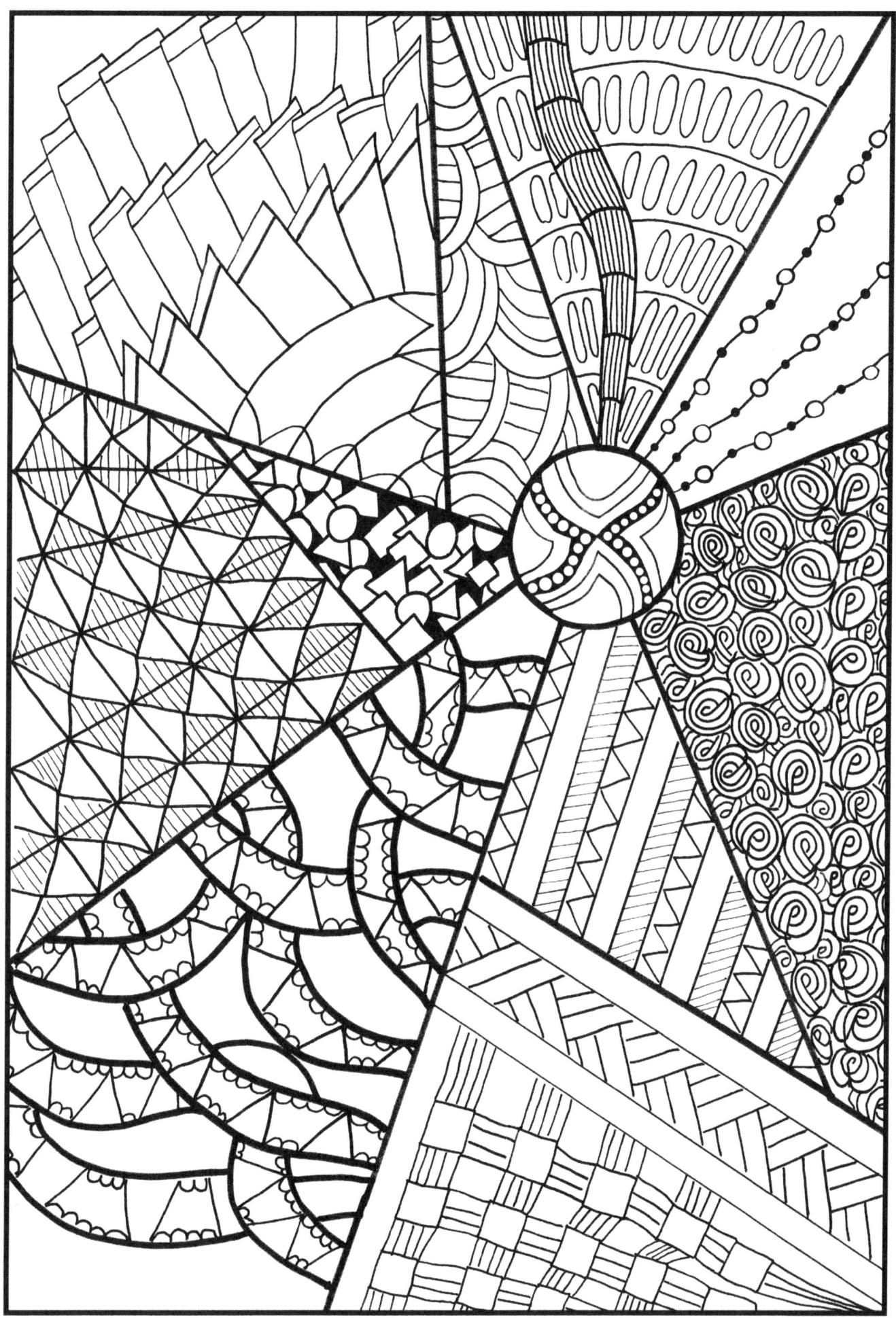

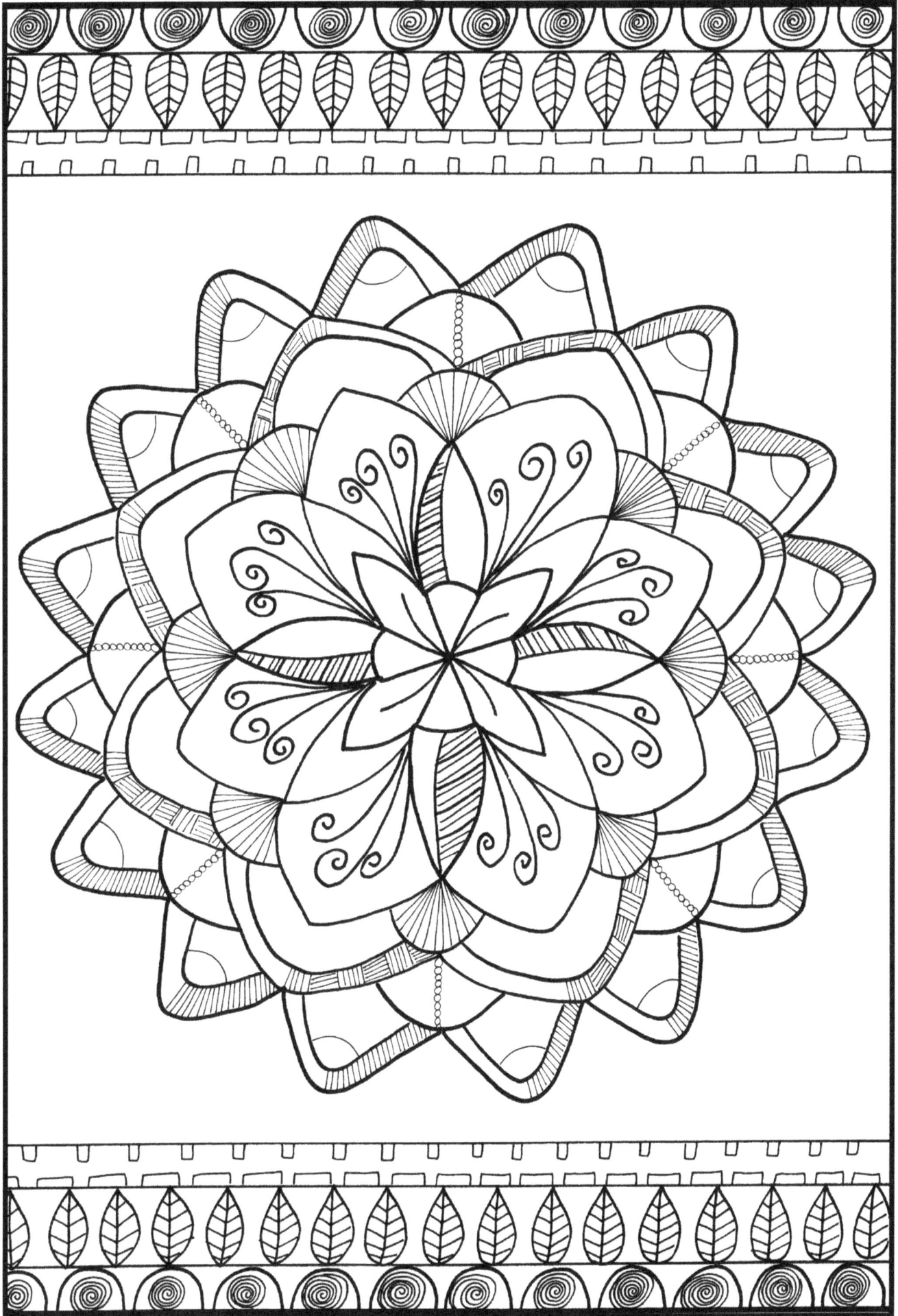

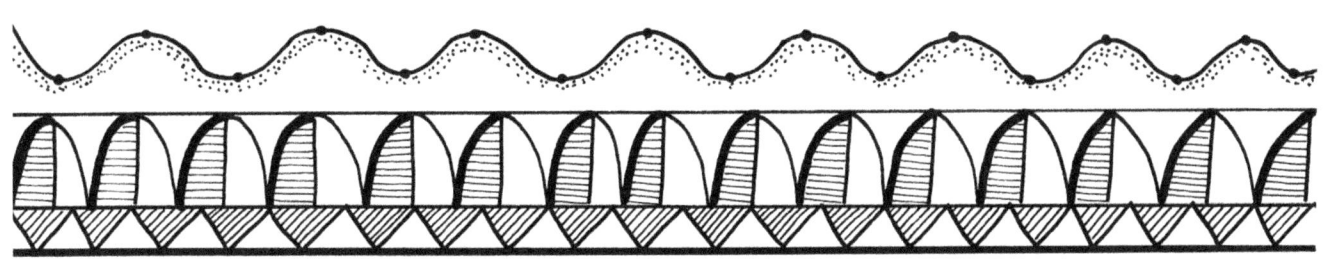
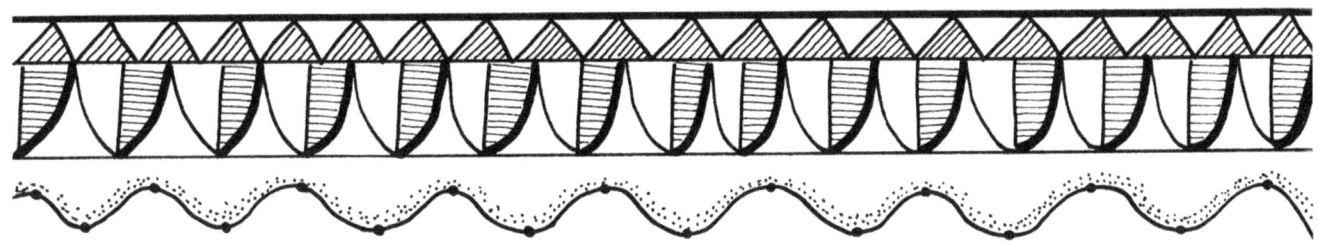

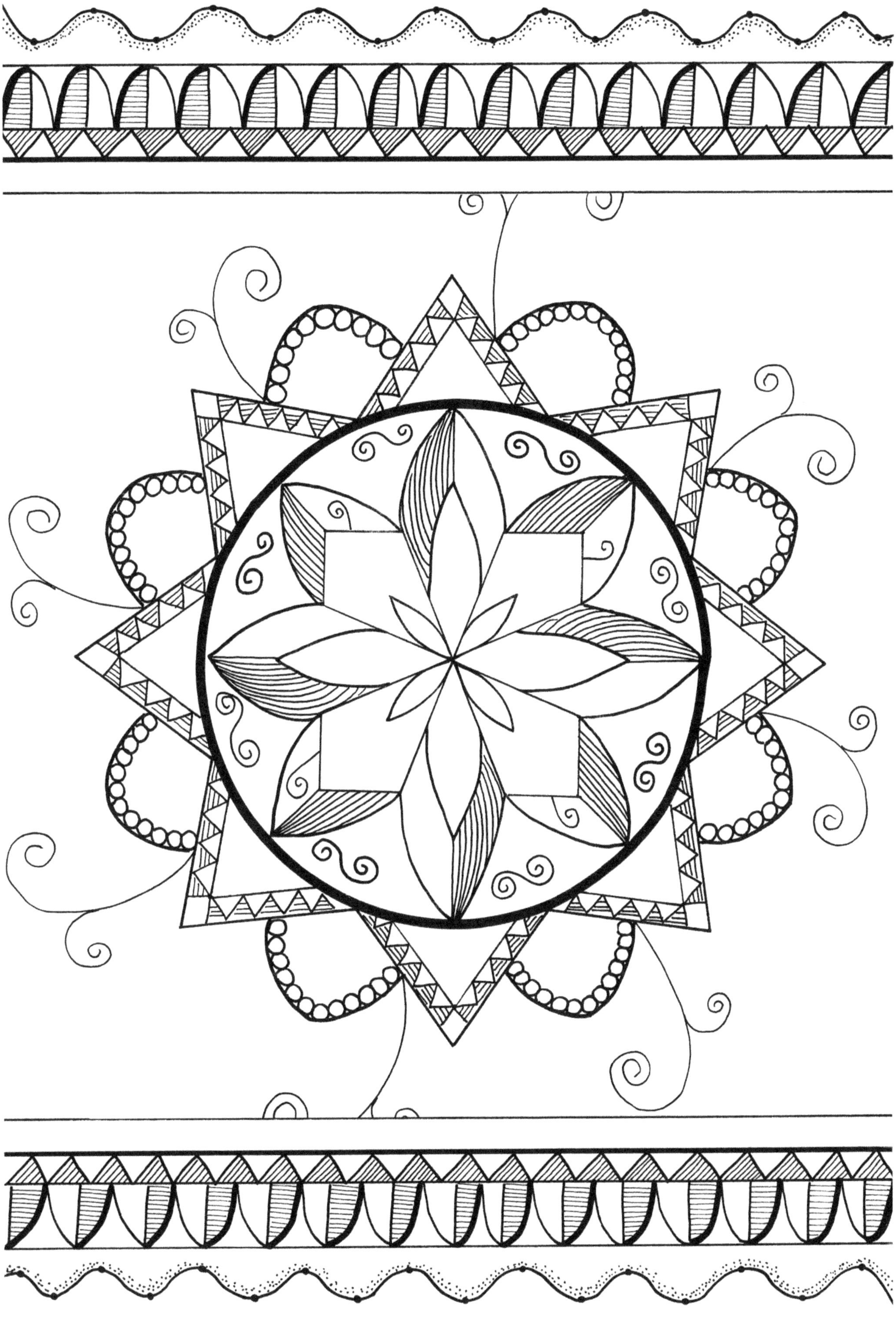

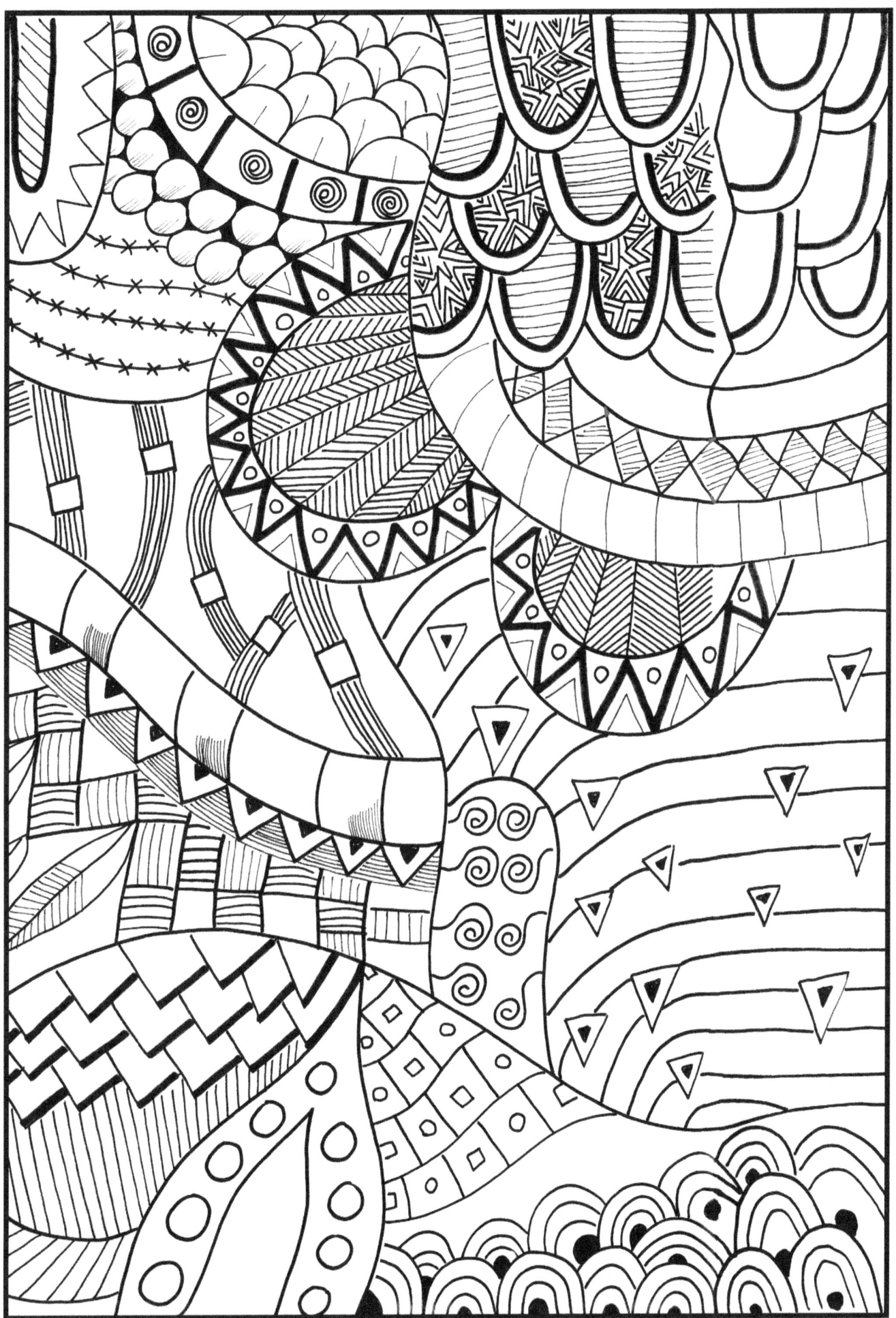

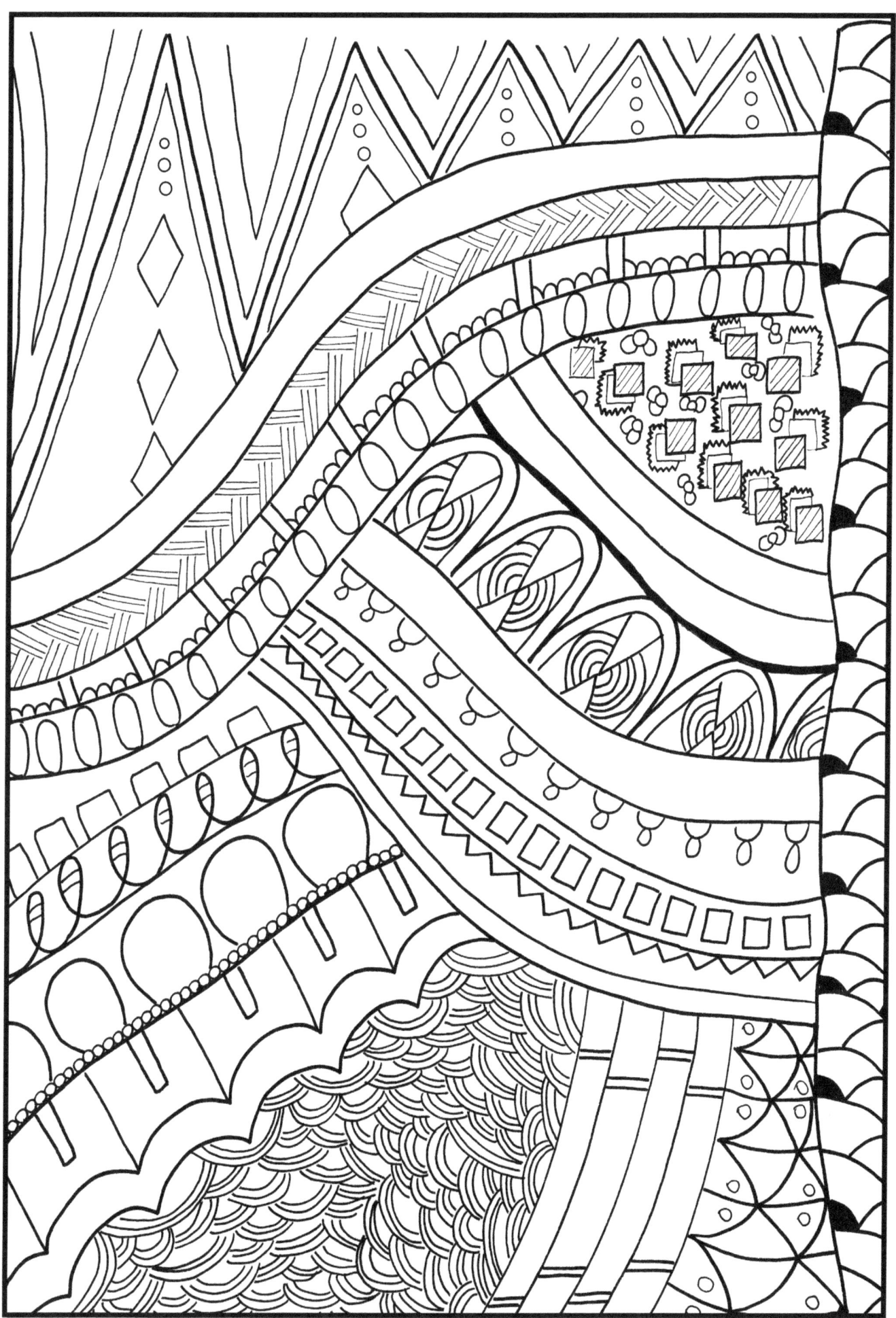

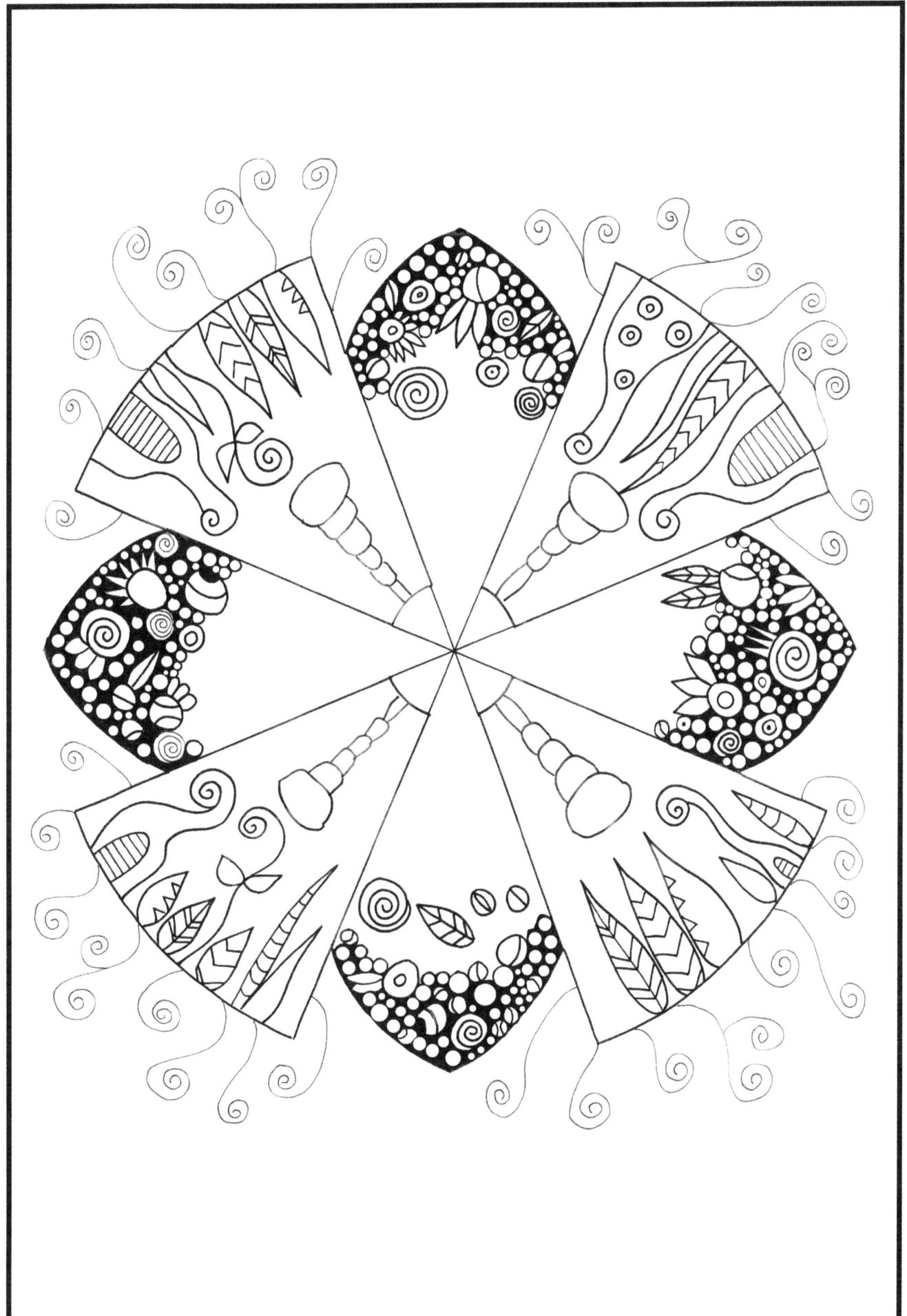

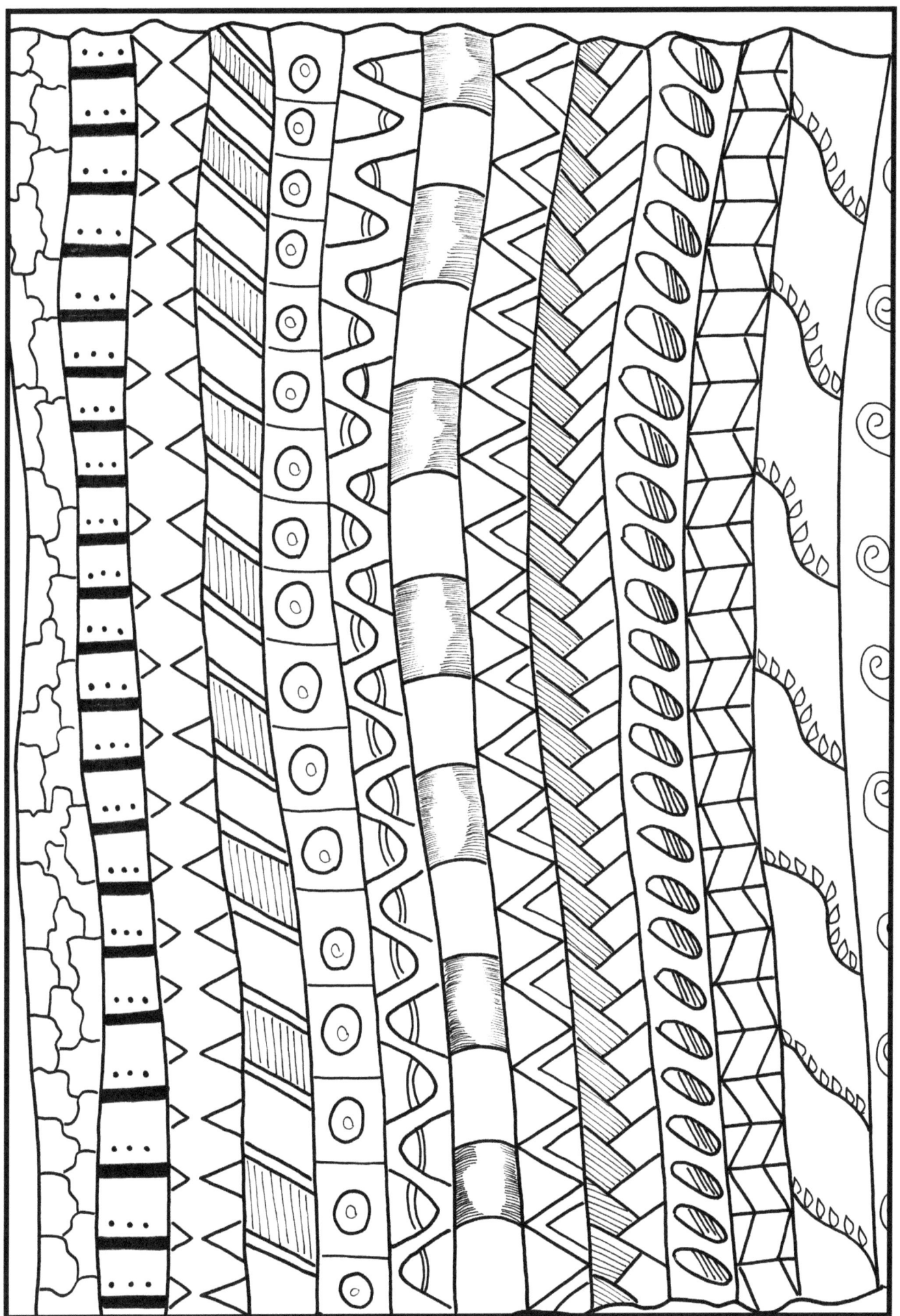

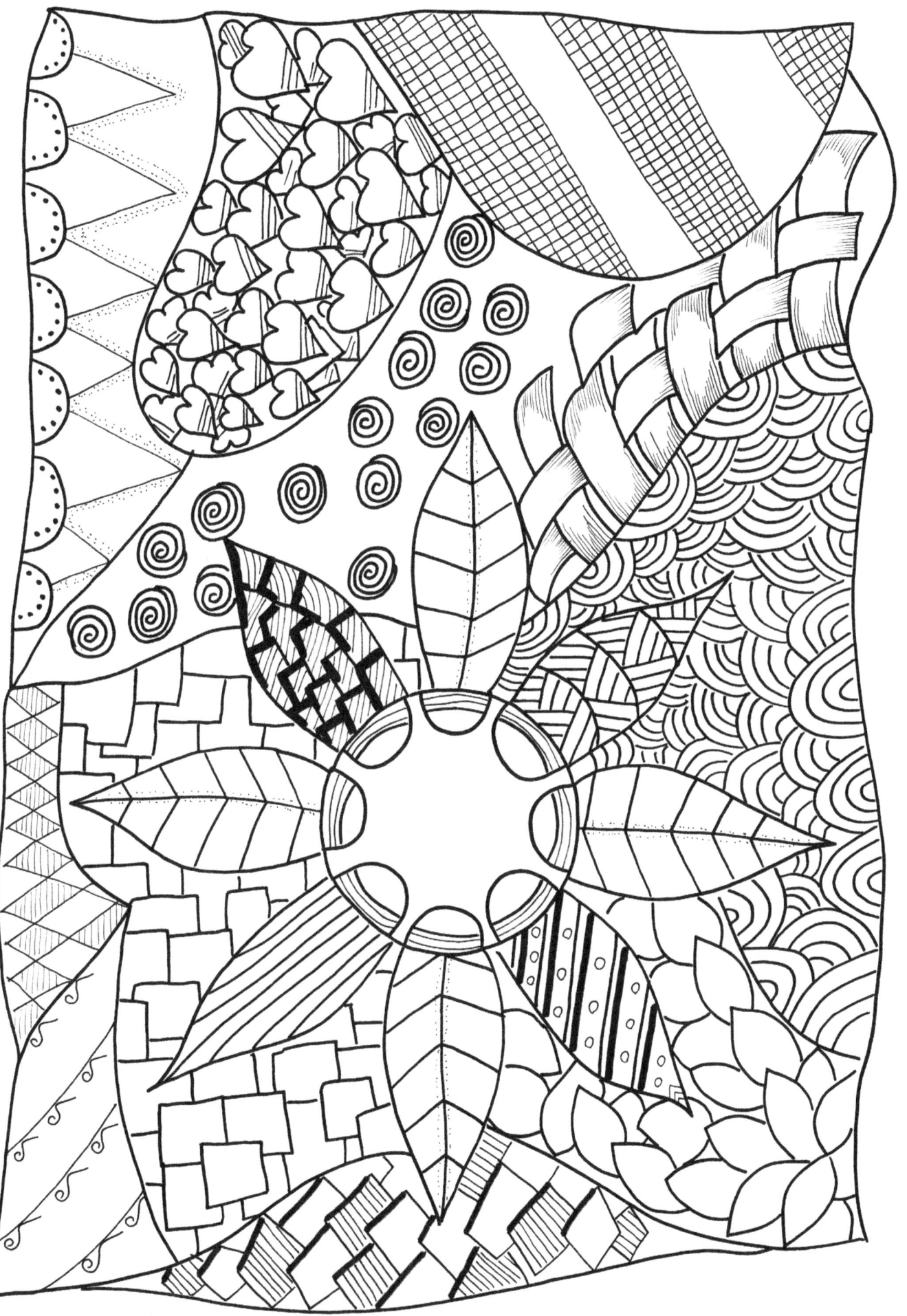

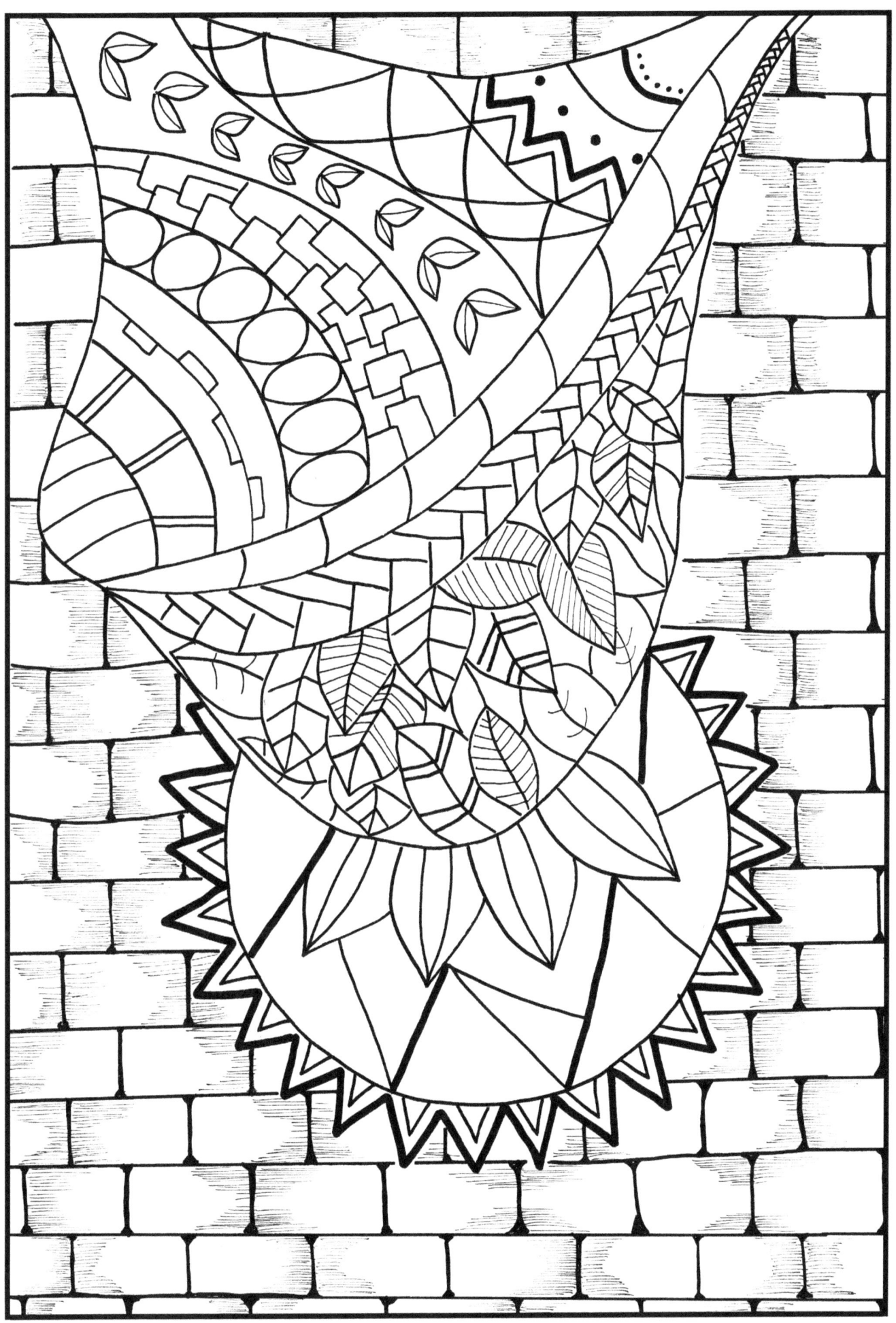

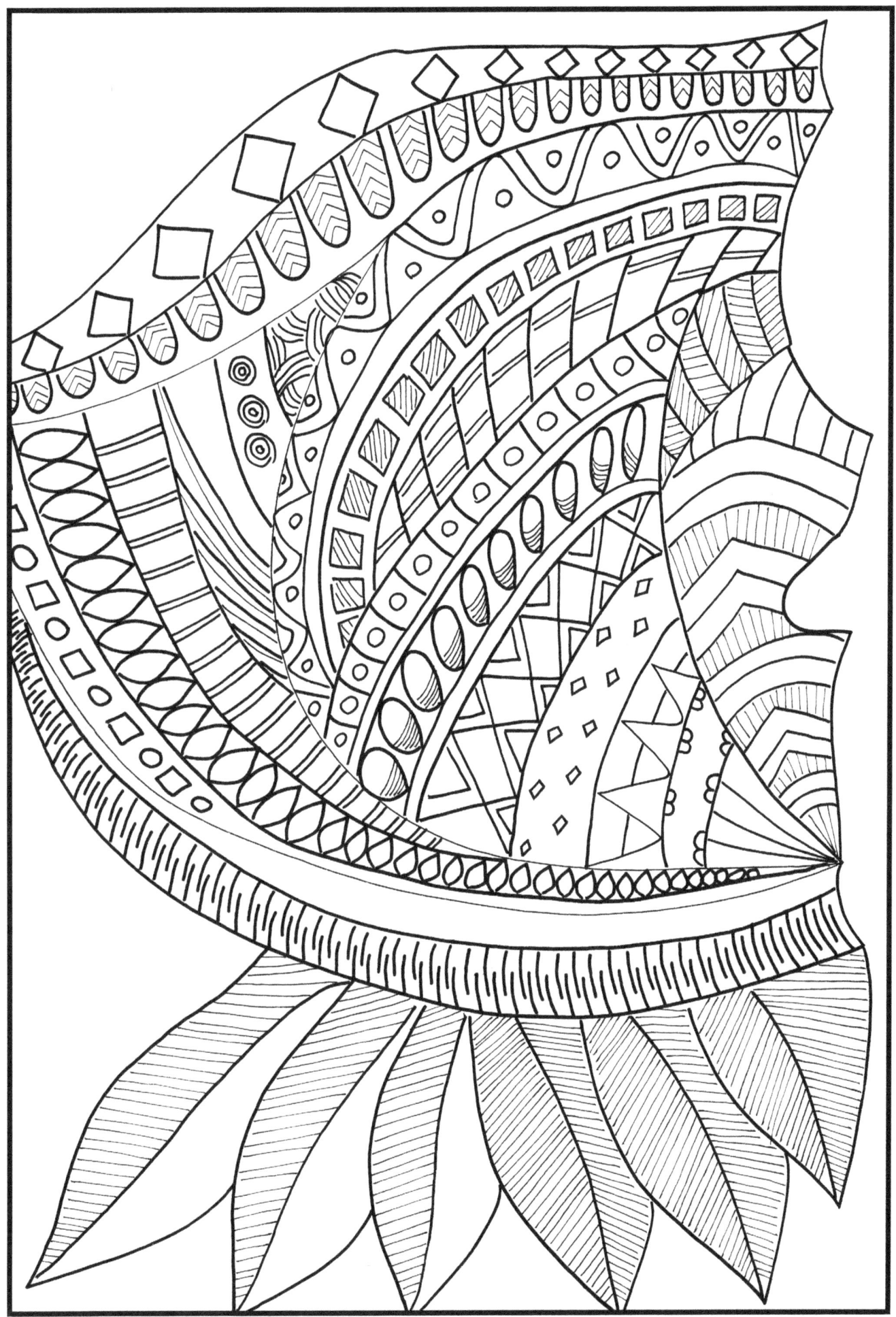

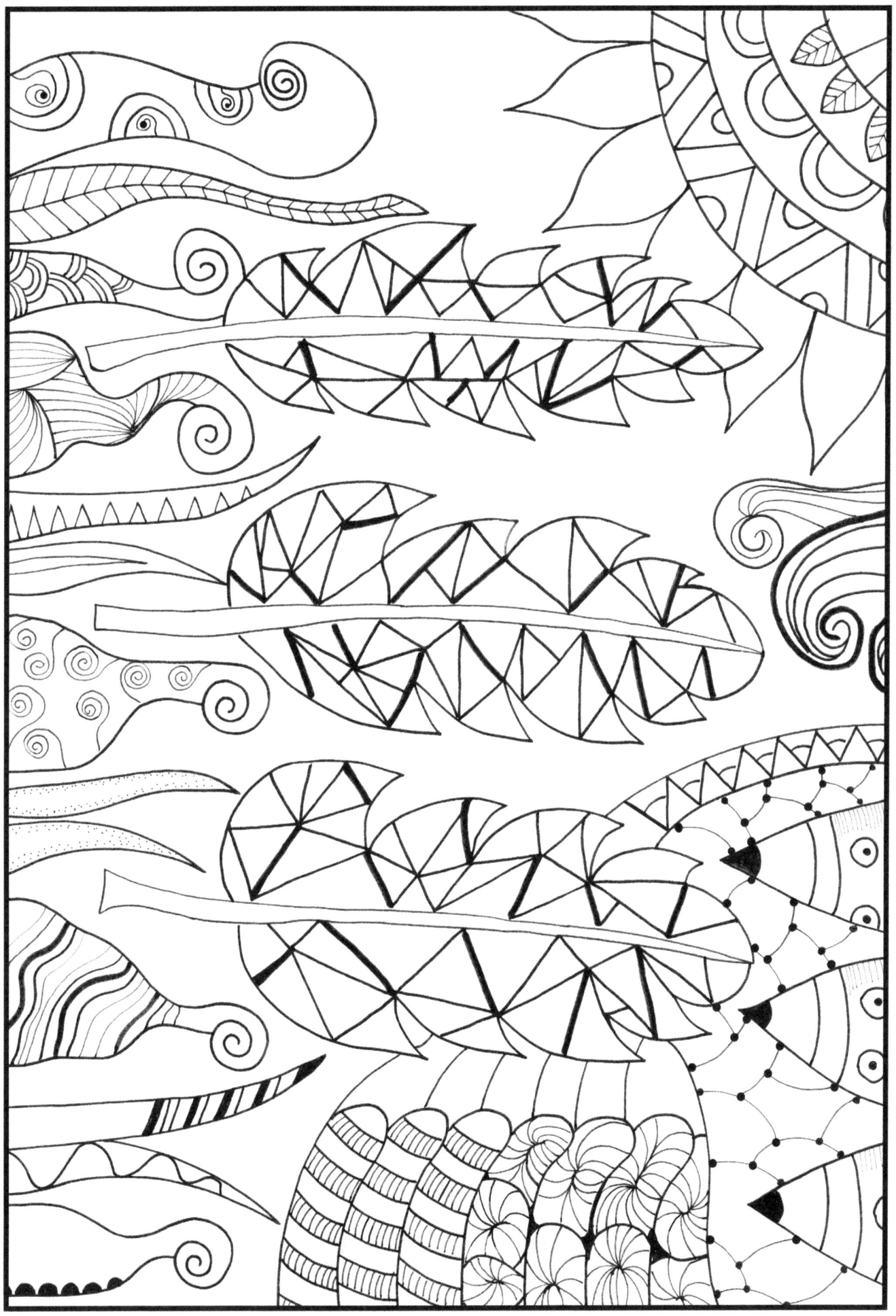

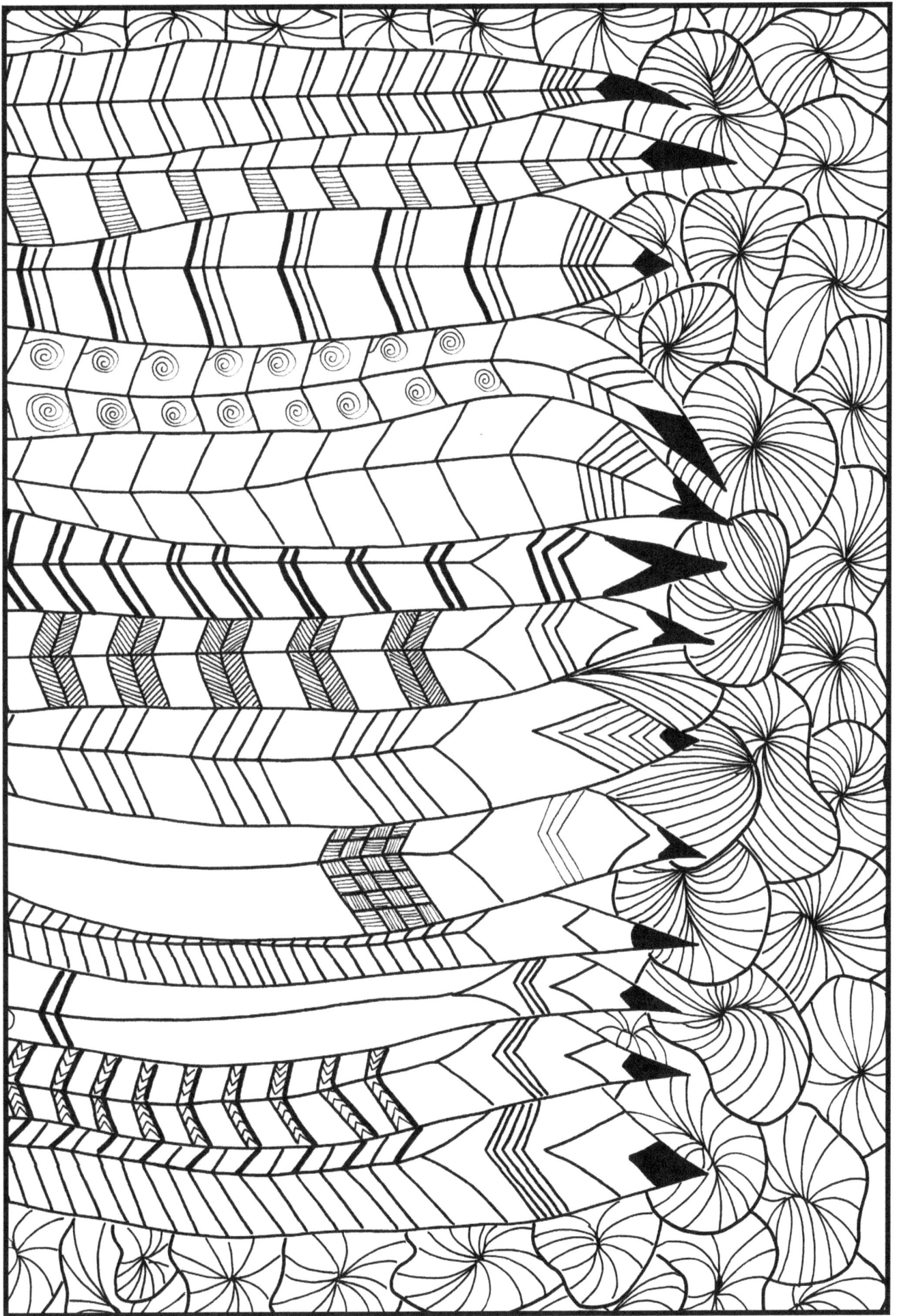

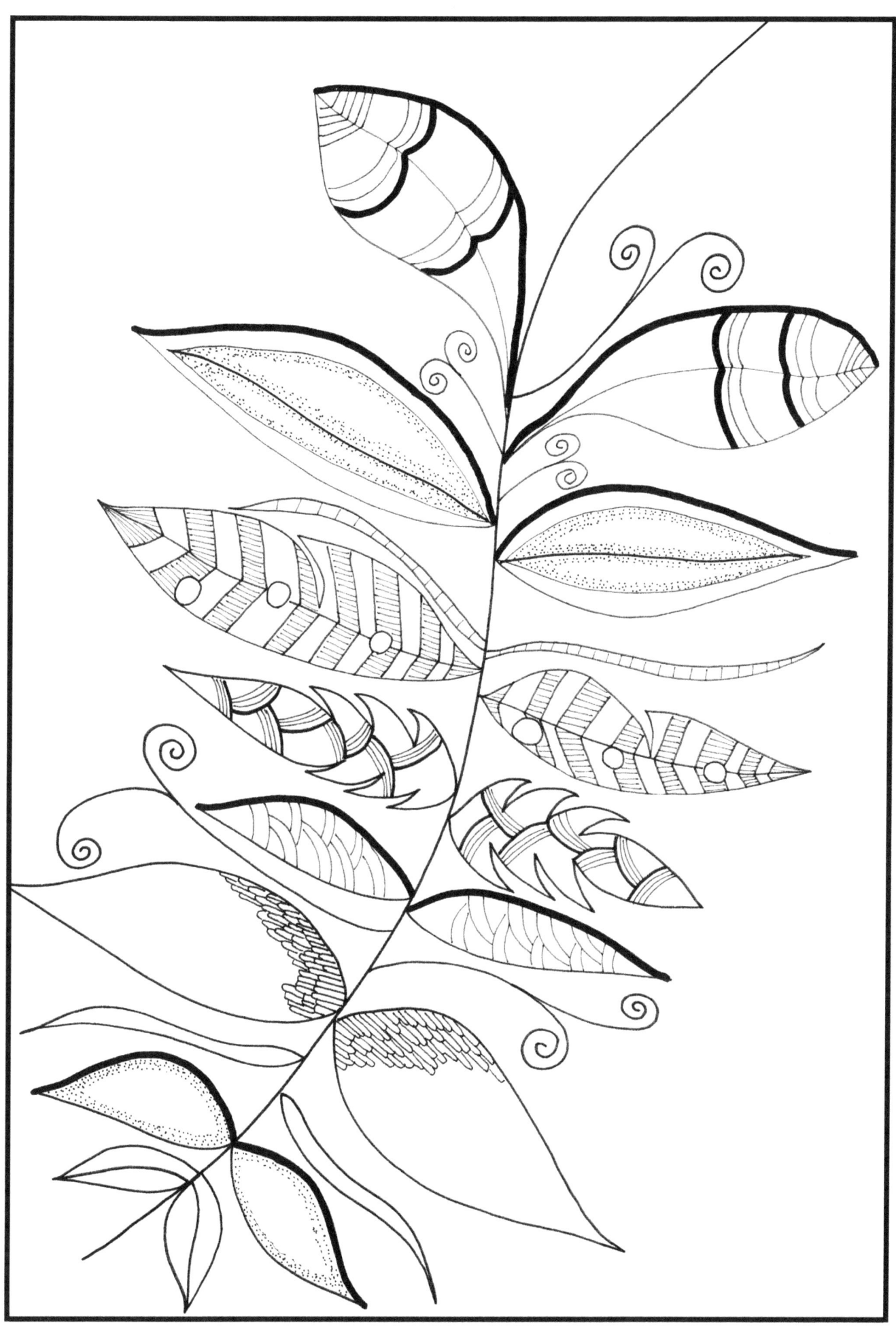

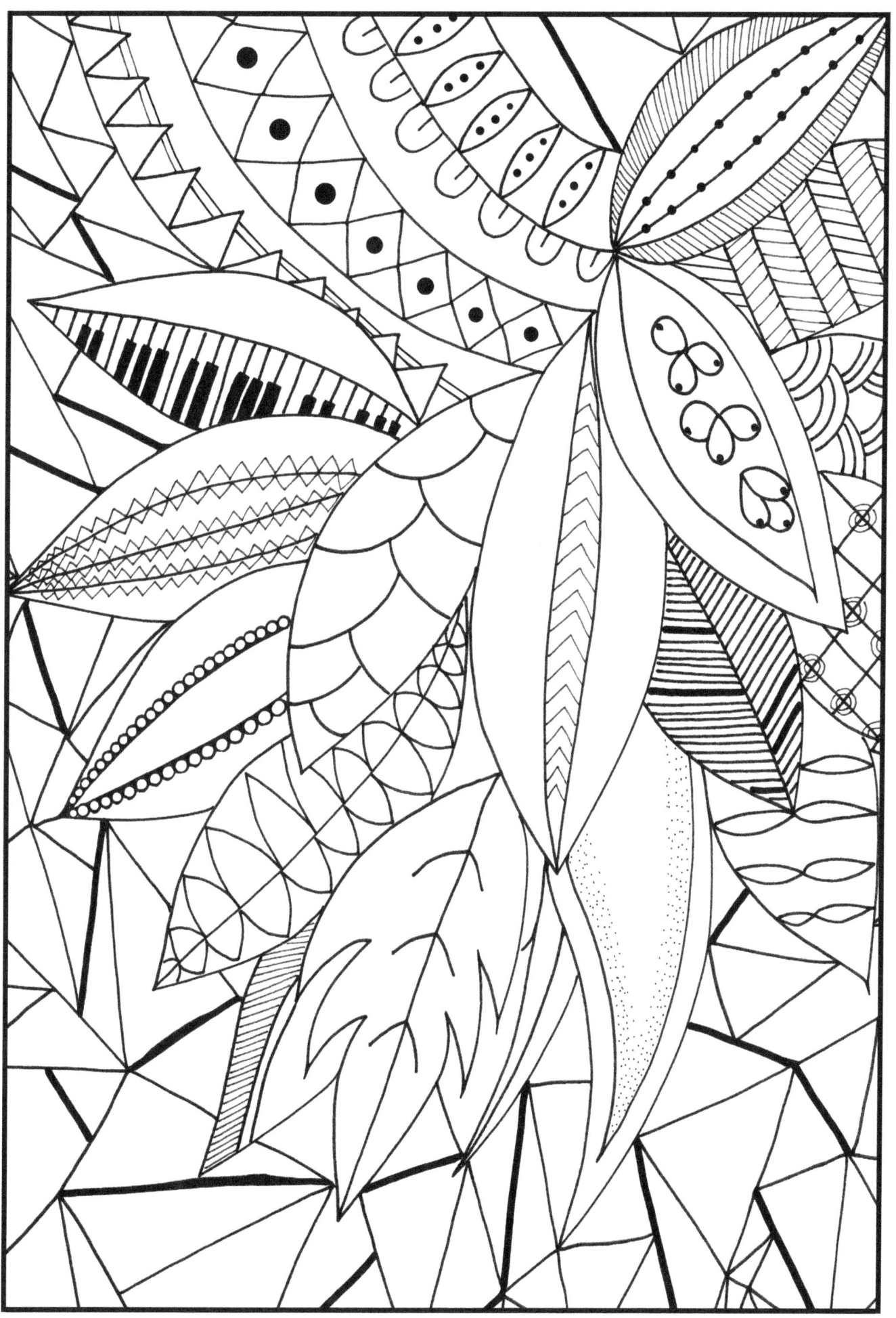

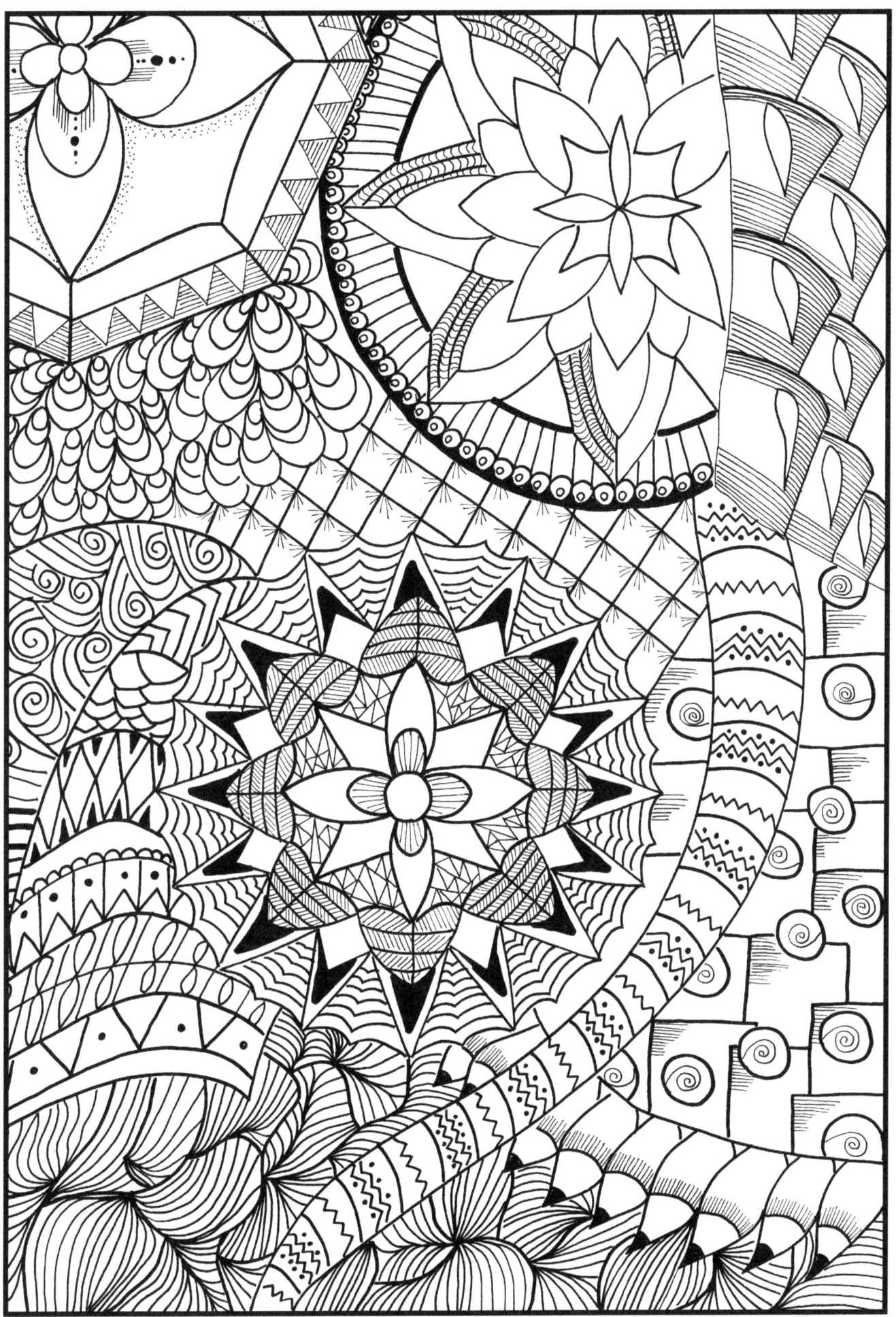

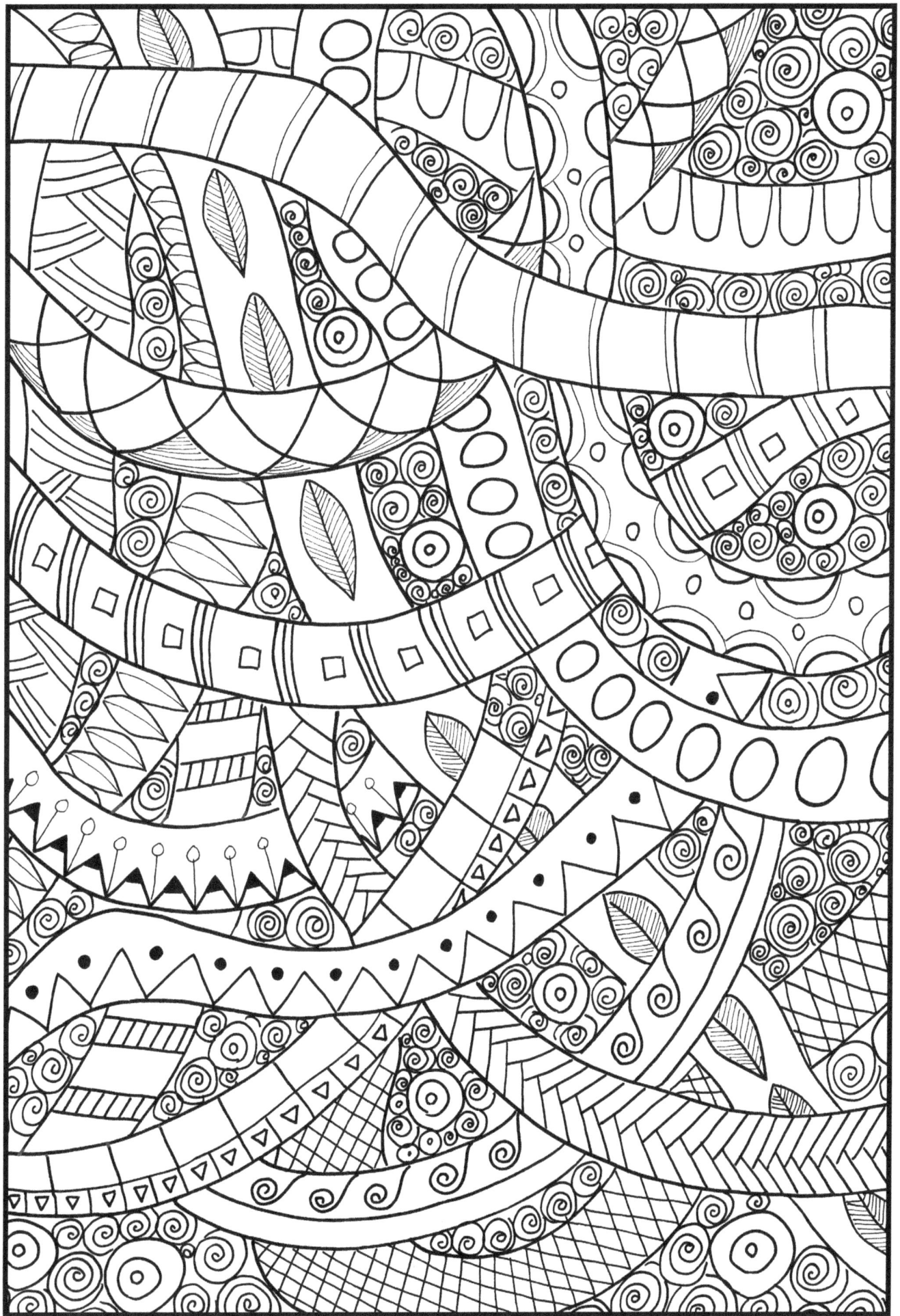

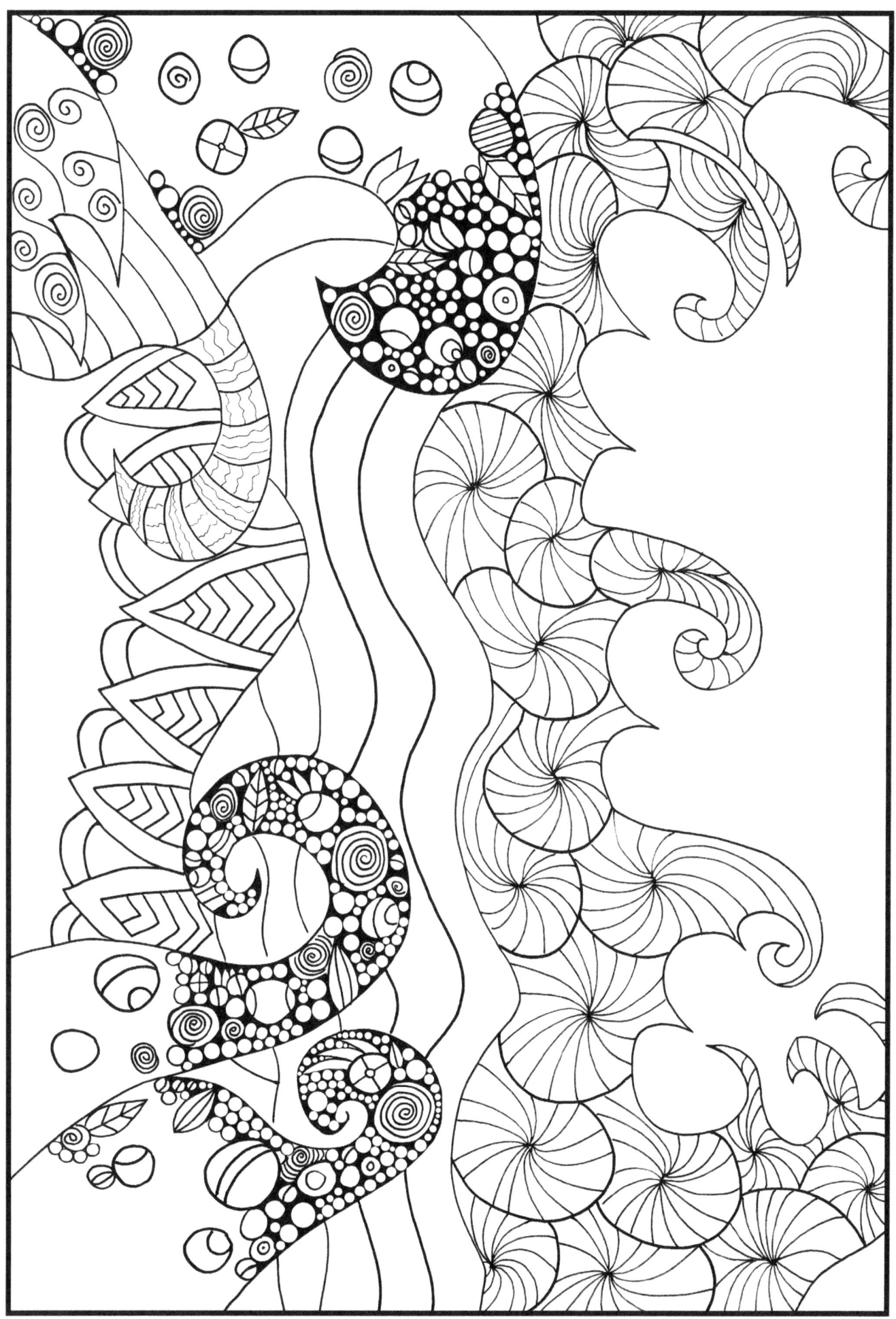

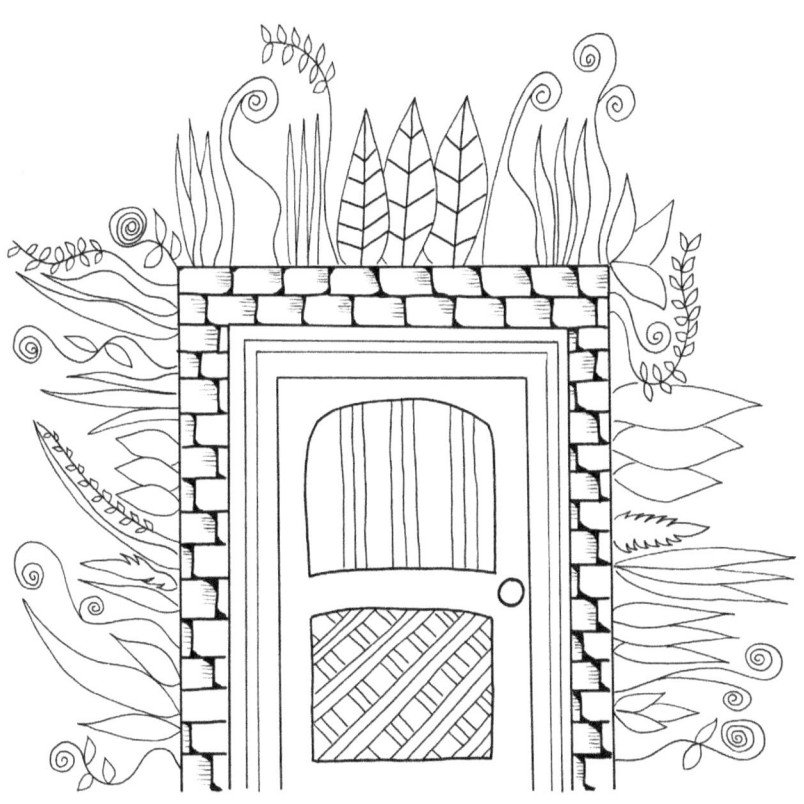

www.ingramcontent.com/pod-product-compliance
Lightning Source LLC
Chambersburg PA
CBHW082302200526
45168CB00017B/2742